NAMING YOUR
BABY

MIMOSA
·BOOKS·

NEW YORK · AVENEL, NEW JERSEY

This 1993 edition published by Mimosa Books, distributed
by Outlet Book Company, Inc., a Random House company,
40 Engelhard Avenue, Avenel, New Jersey 07001

First published in 1991 by Grisewood & Dempsey Ltd.
Copyright © Grisewood & Dempsey Ltd. 1991

10 9 8 7 6 5 4 3 2 1

ISBN 1 85698 512 1

Printed and bound in Italy

INTRODUCTION

Choosing a name is an absorbing and very personal pleasure. The treasury of names is vast and derives from many sources: the Bible, mythology, vernacular names from Old English, French and German, fanciful names dreamed up by Puritans and novelists, Victorian names, cute nicknames adopted as first names, punchy new names from Australia.

In the choice of a name you will undoubtedly be influenced by your last name. You probably wouldn't want to call your daughter Goldie if your surname was Fish, for example. Nor would you want her to have the initials W.E.T.

You might also want the child to have a name with a positive meaning. Would you still want to call your son Gideon if you knew the name meant "having a stump for a hand," or be so eager to name a daughter Kylie if you knew it was Aboriginal for "boomerang"? But there could be refreshing surprises in store, too. How about Azura, meaning "blue skies"?

This book contains more than 2,000 names, some familiar and well-loved, others unusual and exotic. The popularity of some names, like Wendy and Tracy, blazes up and then dies, while others, like John and Jane, go on for centuries. You can opt for fashion or posterity, or you can make a truly original choice.

There is no reason why you should not invent a new name for your child. The Puritans invented names like Prudence (still popular) and Temperance (which fell out of favor quite quickly), and the novelist Margaret Mitchell came up with a whole bouquet of names for *Gone With The Wind* (1936), including Scarlett, Rhett, and Ashley.

Use this book as a prompt for your memory and a springboard for your ideas. Above all, don't rush to pick a name that you or your baby may later regret. A name is a gift for life, and you should select it with love and care.

Aaron (m.) Biblical: the brother of Moses. The name is possibly Egyptian, though the origins are uncertain. The variant forms are Aron and Aharon.

Abel (m.) Biblical: the younger son of Adam and Eve, murdered by his jealous brother Cain. From the Hebrew, meaning "breath," "vapor," hence the name came to mean "worthlessness." The pet forms are Abe, Abie and Nab.

Abigail (f.) Biblical: one of the wives of King David, from the Hebrew meaning "father rejoiced." A popular 17th-century Puritan name, it later came to mean a lady's maid. It is now regaining popularity. The pet forms are Abbie, Abby and Gail, which has become a name in its own right.

Abner (m.) Biblical: King Saul's cousin, and the commander of his army. It comes from the Hebrew meaning "father of light." Uncommon, though still found in parts of the country.

Abraham (m.) Biblical: the Old Testament patriarch. His name was originally Abram, "high father," but God changed it to Abraham, "father of multitudes." Made popular by President Abraham Lincoln (1809-65); the pet forms are Abie, Ham, Bram and Braham. The last two have come to exist as names in their own right.

Ada (f.) Of uncertain origin, possibly a pet form of Adele or Adelaide, it could also be derived from the Old German Eda or Etta, "happy."

Adam (m.) Biblical: the first man, from the Hebrew for "red," possibly because God is said to have fashioned man from clay and then breathed life into him. Many last names come from it (e.g. Atkins, Adcock), and is enjoying a revival as a first name.

Adelaide (f.) From the Old German "noble" and "kind". It became popular in the 19th century when Adelaide of

6

Saxe-Coburg married the English king William IV. The Australian city of Adelaide is named after this queen.

Adele (f.) Pet form of Adelaide, and a name in its own right.

Adrian (m.) From the Latin, "man from Hadria." Hadrian was the great Roman emperor responsible for the building of a wall across Northern England which is named after him. This name has enjoyed popularity only in the last 30 years. Adrianne and Adrienne are feminine forms.

Agatha (f.) From the Greek, "good" or "honorable woman." It was the name of a 3rd-century Sicilian martyr. The name is best known from the crime writer Agatha Christie (1890-1976). The pet form is Aggie.

Agnes (f.) From the Greek, "pure," St. Agnes was a young Roman virgin martyred by Emperor Diocletian, and often portrayed with a lamb (Latin, *agnus*). Another form is Inez, derived from the Spanish. The pet forms are Aggie, Nessie and Nesta.

Ailsa (f.) A modern Scottish name from Ailsa Craig, an island in the Clyde estuary.

Aimeé *see* Amy

Ainsley (m. and f.) Transferred use of a last name, originally meaning "clearing" or "meadow."

Aisling (f.) Pronounced "Ashling"; derived from the Irish Gaelic meaning "dream" or "vision."

Aithne (f.) From the Irish, "little fire." The variants are Ethne, Eithne.

Alan (m.) Either from the Old English for "harmony," or from the Celtic for "rock." Introduced into England with the Norman Conquest; the French forms are Alein and Alain. The variants are Allan, Allen and Alun (Welsh). The name was made more popular by the actor Alan Ladd in the 1950s. The feminine forms are Allana, Alanna and Lana.

Alasdair, Alastair *see* Alexander

Albert (m.) From the Old German meaning "noble" and "bright." It became very popular after the marriage of

Queen Victoria to Prince Albert of Saxe-Coburg in 1840 and has remained in royal currency. The pet forms are Al, Bert and Bertie. The feminine forms, which are quite rare, are Alberta and Albertine (French).

Aldous (m.) From the Old German, "old." Made famous by the novelist Aldous Huxley (1894-1963).

Alec (m.) A shortened form of Alexander, now a name in its own right.

Aled (m.) Welsh, meaning "offspring" or "young one." It is the name of a river in Wales.

Alex (m. and f.) The shortened form of Alexander and Alexandra, it now exists as a name in its own right. Related names are Alix, Alexa, Alexia and Alexis.

Alexander (m.) From the Greek, meaning "defender of men," and made famous by Alexander the Great (356-323 B.C.). In Scotland it is also popular in the forms Alasdair, Alastair, Alistair and Alister. The shortened forms are Alex, Alec, Alick, Alix and Sandy, which are also used as names in their own right.

Alexandra (f.) The feminine form of Alexander (see above). It became popular in the 19th century with the marriage of Princess Alexandra of Denmark to the British Prince of Wales (later King Edward VII). The short forms are Alex, Alexa and Sandra, which have all become names in their own right.

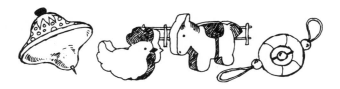

Alfred (m.) From the Old English for "elf" (a good being) and "council." It could also derive from the name Ealdfrith, which means "old peace." The name became famous through the British King Alfred the Great (849-

99). The shortened forms are Alf, Alfie and Fred, and Alfreda is the rare feminine form.

Algernon (m.) From the Norman French, meaning "be-whiskered" or "moustached," it is now rarely used. The pet forms are Algie and Algy.

Alice (f.) From the Old German for "nobility." Most famously the name of Lewis Carroll's heroine in *Alice in Wonderland*, this name has the variants Alicia, Allice, Allyce, Alys and Alyssa. It became firmly established in the 19th century.

Alison (f.) Derived from Alice, this name was popular in the Middle Ages, dying out after that except in Scotland. From about the 1930s it became widespread again. Allison is the alternative spelling. The pet forms are Ally and Allie.

Alistair *see* Alexander

Allegra (f.) From the Italian meaning "cheerful," "happy." The poet Lord Byron gave this name to his illegitimate daughter in 1817.

Alma (f.) Could be derived from the Celtic for "all good," the Latin for "nourishing," the Italian and Spanish for "soul," or the Hebrew for "maiden." It gained popularity after the Battle of Alma in 1854.

Aloysius (m.) Pronounced "Alo-ishus," this is the name of a Spanish saint of the 16th century and could derive from Louis ("famous warrior.").

Althea (f.) From Greek mythology, meaning "wholesome." Used in the 17th century by Richard Lovelace in his lyric *To Althea from Prison*.

Alvin (m.) From the Old English, meaning "noble friend." Recently popular. A Welsh variant is Alwyn.

Amanda (f.) From the Latin for "lovable," this was invented by writers of the 17th century but became popular only in the 20th century. The pet form is Mandy, which has become a name in its own right.

Amaryllis (f.) This was a name used by Greek poets for their pastoral heroines. Possibly it means "sparkling

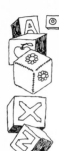

Amber

stream." It was introduced to English verse in the 17th century. It remains uncommon, though it is borne by at least two distinguished musicians.

Amber (f.) From the ornamental fossil resin. First used at the end of the 19th century, this name was made popular by Kathleen Winsor's novel *Forever Amber* (1944).

Ambrose (m.) From the Greek, meaning "immortal" or "divine." The Welsh form is Emrys.

Amelia (f.) A relation of Emily and Amalia, this name comes from the Old German "hardworking." It was used by Henry Fielding in his novel *Amelia* (1751). The pet form is Milly.

Amos (m.) Biblical, from the Hebrew prophet. It derives from the verb meaning "to carry."

Amy (f.) From the Old French meaning "beloved." It became fashionable in the 19th century because of Amy Robsart in Sir Walter Scott's novel *Kenilworth*. It can also be a short form for Annabel.

Anastasia (f.) A Russian name meaning "resurrection," famous in the 20th century from the Tsar's last daughter, whom many believe to be the true embodiment of the name for escaping the massacre of her family in 1917. A popular shortened form is Stacy, which has become a name in its own right.

Andrea (f.) Feminine form of Andrew, especially popular in Scotland. The variants are Andrée (French) and Rena.

Andrew (m.) From the Greek for "warrior," the name was borne by the first disciple to be called by Jesus, and the patron saint of Scotland and Russia. Very popular in Britain, particularly since Queen Elizabeth II gave it to her second son, the Duke of York (b.1960). Pet forms are Andy and Drew, both now names in their own right.

Aneurin (m.) Pronounced "A-nye-rin," this Welsh name

possibly comes from the Latin for "honorable." It is also spelled Aneirin, and the shortened form Nye was made famous by the British Labor politician Aneurin Bevan (1897-1960).

Angela (f.) Comes from the Greek "messenger." Together with its male form, Angel, it was banned by the Puritans, but regained popularity in the 19th century with its variants Angelica, Angelina and Angélique (French). The shortened form is Angie.

Angharad (f.) Very popular in Wales, this derives from the Welsh for "very much loved."

Angus (m.) From the Gaelic for "unique choice." Originally Irish, it has become firmly established in Scotland. The shortened form is Gus.

Anita (f.) The Spanish pet form of Ann, and a name in its own right. The short form is Nita.

Ann(e) (f.) From the Hebrew name Hannah, meaning "grace," it was the name of the mother of the Virgin Mary. Introduced to Britain from France in the 13th century, it has been borne by six queens and continues to be popular with the royal family: Queen Elizabeth II gave it to her only daughter in 1950. The diminutive form Annie is now popular as a name in its own right. Other forms are Nan, Nanette, Nancy, Annette and Anneka. Ann also forms compound names such as Mary Ann (hence Marianne) and Carol Ann. A popular variant is Anna.

Annabel (f.) Probably derives from Amabel, "lovable." Particularly popular in Scotland. The shortened forms are Bel, Belle and Bella, which are also names in their own right, meaning "beautiful."

Anona *see* Ann(e)

Anthea (f.) Greek, meaning "flowery"; this name was introduced into English by the poets of the 17th century, but its use was not widespread until the 20th century.

Anthony (m.) Also spelled Antony, it is a Roman family name, as in Mark Antony. The 'th' was introduced into

11

the name during the Renaissance when scholars assu-
med it was derived from the Greek *anthos*, flower. The
shortened form is Tony, which is a name in its own right
for both sexes, the feminine form being more often
spelled Toni. Antonia is the usual female version, and
Antoinette and Nettie are also found. Anton is gaining
popularity for boys.

Antonia *see* Anthony

April (f.) From the name of the month. It is associated with
the season of the year when buds open; *aperire* is Latin
for "to open."

Arabella (f.) Possibly from the same source as Amabel,
"lovable," and particularly popular in Scotland, where
it is also found as Arabel.

Archibald (m.) A Scottish name derived from the Old
German, meaning "truly bold." The shortened forms
are Archie, Archy and Baldie.

Ariadne (f.) From Greek mythology. Ariadne, the daughter of King Minos of Crete, gave Theseus a thread to
help him find his way out of the labyrinth once he had
killed the Minotaur. The French form Arian(n)e and the
Italian Arian(n)a also appear.

Arlene (f.) Along with Aline, Arleen, Arline, Arlyne and
Arlena, this may have been coined as a variant of
Charlene and Marlene.

Arnold (m.) From the Old German, meaning "eagle ruler."
It came to Britain with the Normans, but fell out of
popularity until the late 19th century. The shortened
forms are Arnie, Arnie and Arn.

Arthur (m.) Could derive from the Welsh word for "bear,"
the Irish for "stone," or be a Roman family name. The
name was spread through Europe with the legends of
King Arthur, about whom few historical facts are known
except that he ruled in the 5th or 6th century. The British
Duke of Wellington, Arthur Wellesley (1769-1852), was
largely responsible for the 19th-century popularity of the
name, together with Queen Victoria's younger son,

Prince Arthur. The shortened form of the name is Art or Artie.

Asa (m.) Biblical: a king of Judah. Means "healer" in Hebrew.

Ashley (m. and f.) A transferred use of the last name meaning "ash wood." It is particularly popular in America and Australia, and increasingly used for girls.

Astrid (f.) From the Scandinavian, meaning "beautiful god," this name has been used in Britain in the 20th century, probably because of the popularity of Astrid, Queen of the Belgians (1905-35).

Athene (f.) From Greek mythology, the goddess of wisdom. She gave her name to the city of Athens. Athena is a variant.

Auberon (m.) Of obscure origin, it is probably related to Aubrey. Its best-known bearer is the British writer, Auberon Waugh. Oberon is a variation.

Aubrey (m.) From German mythology, "the king of the elves." Brought to England with the Norman Conquest, it fell out of popularity until the early years of this century. Other forms are Alberic and Albery.

Audrey (f.) From the Old English name Ethelreda, meaning "noble strength." In the Middle Ages fairs held in honor of St Audrey gave her a bad reputation because the goods sold at them were shoddy or "tawdry", a word coined from her name. The film star Audrey Hepburn (1929-1993) restored the name's popularity. Audra is another form, used particularly in the South, where Audrey also forms compound names, such as Audrey Rose.

Augustus (m.) From the Latin "venerable." Augustine is the diminutive. St. Augustine was the founder of the

Aurelia

Christian Church in England and first Archbishop of Canterbury. The variants are Austen, Austin, Austyn, Ostin and Awstin (Welsh).

Aurelia (f.) From the Latin, "gold." Other related names are Auriol and Oriel.

Aurora (f.) From the Latin, "golden dawn." It is the name of the goddess of the dawn, and latterly of the princess in the ballet *The Sleeping Beauty*. Dawn is the anglicized version of the name.

Austin *see* Augustus

Ava (f.) Of uncertain origin; possibly a variant of Eve. An Old Germanic name that fell out of popularity at the end of the Middle Ages and was made famous this century by the film star Ava Gardner.

Avis (f.) This Norman-French name probably comes from the Latin for "bird." An uncommon name, sometimes also used for men.

Avril (f.) Possibly from the French for "April," or from a 7th-century saint, Everild. Averil is a variant.

Azaria (f.) A 20th-century name which comes from the Hebrew form meaning "helped by God."

B

Babette *see* Elizabeth

Barbara (f.) From the Greek, "strange" or "foreign," the name of a 3rd-century martyr. It fell out of favor after the Middle Ages until this century. A fashionable spelling is now Barbra, after the actress Barbra Streisand (b.1942), and shortened forms are Babs, Bobby and Barbie.

Barnaby (m.) This is a modern version of Barnabas, from the Hebrew for "son of consolation." Barnabas was the name of the disciple who accompanied St. Paul. Barnaby enjoyed popularity in the 19th century with Dickens's novel *Barnaby Rudge* and is now becoming popular again. The short forms are Barney or Barny, which are also short for Bernard.

Barry (m.) From the Irish, meaning "spear." Originally used exclusively in Ireland, this name is now widespread, and particularly popular in Australia. The pet forms are Baz and Bazzer.

Bartholomew (m.) From the New Testament, one of the apostles. The Hebrew form means "son of the furrow," so it was probably originally given to a plowman. Bart and Barth are the short forms.

Basil (m.) From the Greek, "royal," it was brought to England during the Crusades. The shortened forms are Bas, Baz and Bazzer.

Beatrice (f.) From the Latin, "bringer of joy." Famous as the name of Dante's heroine, it has royal connections in England since being chosen by Queen Victoria for her youngest daughter, and by the present Duke and Duchess of York for their eldest (b.1988). The pet forms are Bee, Bea, Trixie and Beatty. Another spelling is Beatrix, as in the children's writer Beatrix Potter.

Becky (f.) A shortened form of Rebecca that also exists as a name in its own right. Becky Sharp was Thackeray's heroine in *Vanity Fair* (1874).

Belinda (f.) Of uncertain origin. It first became popular in the 18th century when it was used in plays by Vanbrugh and Congreve and in Alexander Pope's poem *The Rape of the Lock*. Short forms are Linda, Bel and Lindy.

Bella (f.) Italian for "beautiful." Bella is also short for Arabella and Isabella. Belle is the French equivalent.

Benedict (m.) From the Latin, "blessed." St. Benedict (c.480 – c.550) founded the Benedictine monastic order. Alternative forms are Benedick and Bennett. The name is especially popular in Roman Catholic families.

Benjamin (m.) Biblical. Benjamin was the youngest of

15

Jacob's 12 sons, and the founder of one of the 12 tribes of Israel. His mother, Rachel, died giving birth to him. The name is possibly from the Hebrew meaning "son of my right hand," or "son of strength." The name is currently popular. Its shortened forms are Ben, Benjie, and Benny.

Berenice (f.) From the Greek, "bringer of victory." Also spelled Bernice, its shortened forms are Berry, Berny and Bunny.

Bernadette (f.) The feminine form of Bernard. Very popular in Ireland, where it is given in Roman Catholic families in honor of St. Bernadette of Lourdes.

Bernard (m.) From the Old German words for "bear" and "strong," the name implies "brave." Three saints bore it, including St. Bernard of Menthon (923-1008), who founded hospices on the alpine passes and gave his name to St. Bernard dogs. Short forms are Bernie, Barny and Bunny.

Berry (f.) A 20th-century name, after the fruit.

Bert (m) The short form of Albert, Bertram, Herbert and similar names.

Bertram (m.) From the Old German meaning "bright raven." Bert and Bertie are the diminutives, and a variant is Bertrand, as in the philosopher Bertrand Russell (1872-1970).

Beryl (f.) Taken from the gemstone, this name became popular in the 19th century.

Bess *see* Elizabeth

Beth (f.) A shortened form of Elizabeth, ("oath of God") and popular as a name in its own right, especially since Louisa M. Alcott gave the name to one of her heroines in *Little Women* (1868). It is also a shortened form of the Hebrew name Bethia.

Bethany (f.) From the New Testament, the name of the village where Lazarus lived. Becoming very popular.

Bettina (f.) A shortened form of the Italian version of Elizabeth, now popular as a name in its own right.

Betty *see* Elizabeth

Beulah (f.) Biblical, from the Hebrew for "married."

Beverl(e)y (f.) From the Old English, meaning "of the beaver stream." It is also used as a boy's name.

Bianca (f.) From the Italian, "white." Famously borne by Bianca Jagger, model and peace worker and former wife of the Rolling Stone, Mick Jagger.

Bill *see* William

Billie (f.) Sometimes spelled Billy, this pet form of the boy's name William is now becoming popular for girls, especially in America, where it forms compound names, as in Billie Jean King, the tennis champion.

Blair (m. and f.) A Scottish name, meaning "flat land," it has been transferred from use as a last name.

Blaise (m.) From the Latin, meaning "stammerer." It is also spelled Blaze and Blase.

Blake (m.) Originally meaning "black" or "of dark complexion" in Old English, this last name is now becoming a popular first name.

Blanche (f.) Comes from the French meaning "white" or "fair."

Bob *see* Robert

Bobbie, Bobby (m. and f.) Pet forms of Robert ("fame" and "bright") and Roberta, and increasingly used in their own right.

Bonnie, Bonny (f.) In Scottish the name means "beautiful." Bonnie Parker, gangster partner of Clyde Barrow, is possibly responsible for the popularity of the name since 1967, the year of the film *Bonnie and Clyde*.

Boris (m.) From the Russian, "fight."

Brenda (f.) From the Old Norse, "sword." It became

Brendan

popular in the 19th century after Sir Walter Scott used it in one of his novels.

Brendan (m.) From the Celtic, "prince." It is particularly popular in Ireland after the 6th-century saint. The variants are Brandon and Brendon.

Brent (m.) Transferred use of the last name, meaning "hill" in Old English.

Brett (m.) Transferred use of the last name, meaning "a Breton." Like Brent, it has become popular over the last couple of decades.

Brian (m.) Old Celtic for "hill," "high" or "strength." It has long been particularly popular in Ireland because of the 10th-century hero King Brian Boru. The alternative spellings are Brien, Bryan and Bryon.

Bridget (f.) This derives from the same Old Celtic origins as Brian. It is very popular in Ireland, being the name of one of its patron saints, St. Bridget of Kildare. The variants are Brigid, Brigit and Brigitte (French). The pet forms are Biddie and Bridie.

Briony (f.) From the plant, one of a group of 19th-century flower names. It can also be spelled Bryony.

Bronwen (f.) From the Welsh meaning "white breast." Popular in Wales.

Brooke (f.) Transferred use of the last name, meaning "brook." Made popular by the actress Brooke Shields.

Bruce (m.) The Scottish last name, originally from Normandy, now popular as a first name, particularly in Scotland and Australia.

Bruno (m.) From Germanic origins, "brown."

Bryn (m.) A 20th-century Welsh name, meaning "hill."

Bunty (f.) A traditional name for a pet lamb, it was first used for girls after the success of a play called *Bunty Pulls the Strings* (1911).

Burt (m.) A name in its own right, a variant of Bert, which is short for Albert, Bertram and similar names.

C

Caitlin (f.) The Irish form of Catherine ("pure").

Caleb (m.) Biblical, from the Hebrew for "dog, dogged." Used in North America and Scotland.

Calum (m.) A Gaelic form of the Latin given name Columba, "dove." Pet forms are Cally or Caley, and the feminine is Calumina.

Calvin (m.) Originally Old French, "bald," it was the last name of the Protestant reformer Jean Calvin (1509-64) and has since been used as a boy's name.

Cameron (m.) Transferred use of the last name, originally meaning "crooked nose". Recently popular as a first name, especially in Scotland.

Camilla (f.) An old Roman family name, given by Virgil to one of his heroines. It became popular in the 18th century as the title of a novel by Fanny Burney (Madame d'Arblay); and the French version of the name, Camille, was the title of a Greta Garbo film in the 1930s.

Campbell (m.) Transferred use of a Scottish family name, originally meaning "crooked mouth." Recently popular as a first name, particularly in Scotland.

Candice (f.) An ancient title belonging to the queens of Ethiopia, it has been used as a first name since the 17th century. It recently became famous because of the actress Candice Bergen. The variants are Candace and Candis, and the pet form is Candy.

Candida (f.) From the Latin, "white," and associated with purity. It was hardly used before the early 20th century, and then probably as a result of George Bernard Shaw's play *Candida* (1898).

Cara (f.) From the Italian, "beloved." Also spelled Kara. Carita and Carina are diminutives.

Carey (m. and f.) This is a transferred use of the last name. The variant spelling is Cary, which was made famous by the film star Cary Grant.

19

Carl (m.) From the Old German, "man," and the origin of Charles. Both the masculine and the feminine form, Carla, are becoming increasingly popular; they can also be spelled with a "K." Carly is a feminine variant.

Carmel (f.) Hebrew, "garden" or "orchard." The name of a mountain near Haifa in Israel traditionally visited by Mary and the infant Jesus where St. Louis founded a church. The variants are Carmela and Carmelita.

Carmen (f.) Latin, "song." A Spanish name which spread in use because of Bizet's opera of the same name (1875).

Carol (f. and m.) This was originally a boy's name from the same source as Carl and Charles, but is now most often a girl's name. The alternative spellings are Carole, Caryl and Carroll. A variant is Carola.

Caroline (f.) A female variation from the same root as Charles. It can also be spelled Carolyn or Carolyne, and a variant is Carolina. The pet forms are Carrie, Caro, Caddie, and Lyn.

Carys (f.) A 20th-century Welsh name from the word for "love."

Casey (m. and f.) This could come from Casimir, "proclaimer of peace," or from a Celtic word meaning "valor." Casey Jones (1863-1900), the engineer who died to save the lives of his passengers, got his name from Cayce, the town in Kentucky where he was born.

Cassandra (f.) The name of a princess of Troy, a prophetess who was never believed. It comes from the Greek meaning "helper of men." Popular in the Middle Ages, the name has enjoyed a recent revival. The short forms are Cass and Cassie.

Catherine *see* Katharine

Catriona (f.) A Scottish variant of Katharine ("pure"), and the title of a novel by Robert Louis Stevenson (1893), which made it widely popular.

Cecil (m.) Transferred use of a noble family name, it derives from the Latin, "blind."

Cecilia (f.) The feminine of Cecil. St. Cecilia is the patron saint of music. There are many variants: Cecily, Cecile, Cicely, Sisley and Cecil. The shortened forms are Cissie, Cissy, Ciss, Sis and Sissy.

Cedric (m.) This was coined by Sir Walter Scott for his novel *Ivanhoe* (1819). It is probably a variant of Cerdic, a Saxon king of Wessex.

Celia (f.) Originally from the Latin, "heavenly," it was brought to light by Shakespeare in *As You Like It*.

Charlene (f.) A 20th-century feminine form of Charles, this is particularly used in America and Australia. It can also be spelled Charline, Charleen and Sharleen.

Charles (m.) From the Old German, "man." A favorite British royal name since the 17th century, the variant forms are Charlie, Chas, Chuck (North America), and Chay (Scotland). It has been particularly popular since it was given to the heir to the British throne in 1948.

Charlotte (f.) The feminine form of the Italian version of Charles, Carlo. It became popular with Queen Charlotte, wife of King George III (married 1761), and is now enjoying a revival. The pet forms are Lottie, Charlie and Charley.

Charmian (f.) From the Greek, "delight." Charmian was one of Cleopatra's attendants. A modern version is Charmaine, made popular by the 1920s song and its revival in the 1950s.

Chelsea (f.) An old English word for port, or landing place. Popular from 1960s pop culture and President Clinton's daughter.

Cherry (f.) An abbreviated form of the 17th-century virtue name Charity. It can also be taken to come from the French for "darling," or from the fruit.

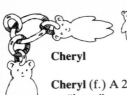

Cheryl

Cheryl (f.) A 20th-century Welsh name, from the word for "love."

Chester (m.) Transferred use of the last name; the pet name is Chet.

Chloë (f.) From the Greek, "tender plant," this name is becoming increasingly popular.

Christabel (f.) From the Latin, "beautiful Christian."

Christian (m. and f.) From the Latin, "follower of Christ." It was used mainly for boys after 1684, when John Bunyan gave it to the hero of *Pilgrim's Progress*.

Christine (f.) From the Latin, "Christian." The variants are Christiana, Christina, Chris, Chrissy, Christy, Kristina, Kirsty (Scotland), Kristen and Kirsten (Scandinavia).

Christopher (m.) From the Greek, "bearing Christ." Popular among early Christians and taken literally in the legend of St. Christopher, who is supposed to have carried the Christ child over a river, making him the patron saint of travelers. Short forms are Chris, Kris and Kit. Christy is used in Ireland.

Cindy (f.) The short form of Lucinda ("light"), now a name in its own right and especially popular in North America. It is also spelled Sindy.

Clare, Claire, Clara (f.) From the Latin, "bright," "clear." Several Italian saints have borne this name, most notably Clare of Assisi, who founded the order of the Poor Clares. Claribel and Clarinda are variants; Clarrie is a pet form.

Clarice, Clarissa (f.) Clarice is the older name, from the Latin, "famous," but Clarissa took over in popularity after the publication of Samuel Richardson's novel *Clarissa* (1748).

Claudia (f.) From the old Roman family name Claudius, which is derived from the word for "lame." Claude, Claudette and Claudine are French forms, and Claud and Claude are the masculine form, not much used today.

Clementine (f.) The feminine form of Clement, from the

Latin for "merciful." Clementina is also found for girls and Clem and Clemmie for both girls and boys.

Cleo (f.) Short for Cleopatra, meaning "glory" or "father's fame," from the famous Egyptian queen who was the lover of Mark Antony and died in 30 B.C. A variant is Clio.

Clifford (m.) From the place name, meaning "a ford at a slope." The short form is Cliff, which became popular from the 1960s with singer Cliff Richard.

Clint (m.) The shortened form of Clinton, a place name, meaning "headland farm." It gained fame through film star Clint Eastwood (b.1930).

Clive (m.) From a place name, meaning "cliff." A last name, first used as a given name in the 19th century by the novelist Thackeray in *The Newcomes*, perhaps with Sir Robert Clive (Clive of India) in mind.

Clyde (m.) From the river in Scotland. It was given a boost in popularity by the film *Bonnie and Clyde* (1967).

Colin (m.) Short form of Nicholas ("victory to the people"), and for 700 years a name in its own right. Also, Gaelic for "young dog."

Colleen (f.) From the Irish, "girl," it is popular in North America and Australia.

Conrad (m.) From the Old German, "bold counsel."

Constance (f.) From the Latin, "constancy." Introduced into England with the Norman Conquest, it appeared as Custance in the Middle Ages and Constantia in the 19th century. The short forms are Connie and Con.

Cora (f.) From the Greek, "maiden." Used in England since the early 19th century, it is nowadays more popular in America.

Coral (f.) One of a group of late 19th-century jewel names. A variation is Coralie.

Cordelia

Cordelia (f.) Of obscure origin, this name first appeared as Cordeilla and was altered to its present form by Shakespeare, who gave it to King Lear's one virtuous daughter.

Corinne (f.) From the Greek, "maiden." Corinna is also found for a girl, and Corin for a boy, as in the actor, Corin Redgrave.

Courtney (m. and f.) The transferred use of a French family name.

Craig (m.) The transferred use of a Scottish last name, from the Gaelic, "crag".

Cressida (f.) From a legendary Trojan princess of bad character. The name has recently become popular. Its short form is Cressy.

Crispin (m.) From a Roman family name, meaning "curly-headed," two Latin forms of the name were borne by the 3rd-century patron saints of shoemakers, Crispinus and Crispinianus.

Crystal (f.) One of a group of 19th-century jewel names, and popular in North America. A variant is Krystle. The name has the connotations of purity and clarity.

Cynthia (f.) One of the titles of the Greek goddess Artemis, who was supposed to have been born on Mount Cynthos.

Cyril (m.) From the Greek, "lord." The name of the 9th-century Greek saint who brought Christianity to the Slavs of Eastern Europe. In order to translate the gospels he devised the Cyrillic alphabet.

D

Daisy (f.) From the name of the flower, "day's eye," because the yellow of the sun appears in the morning and disappears at sundown when the petals close over it. It is also a pet name for Margaret, because Marguerite is the French equivalent of Daisy.

Dale (m. and f.) A transferred use of the last name, meaning "valley." In America, it is frequently now given to girls as well as boys.

Damian (m.) From the Greek, "to tame" or "to subdue (if necessary by killing)." Popular over the past couple of decades, the variant forms are Damien, Damon and Damion.

Dana (f. and m.) The masculine form comes from the Old English for "Dane," and the feminine form derives from the Celtic goddess of fertility.

Daniel (m.) From the Hebrew for "God is my judge." The prophet Daniel was the slave of Nebuchadnezzar. He interpreted the king's dreams, was thrown into the lion's den, and saved by God. Short forms are Dan and Danny, and the feminine forms are Danielle and Daniella.

Daphne (f.) Greek, "laurel." It was the name of a nymph who, fleeing from the attentions of Apollo, called on the gods to help her escape, which they did by turning her into a laurel bush. It was popular for dogs until the early 20th century, when it became a first name for girls. The short forms are Daff and Daffy.

Darren (m.) Of uncertain origin, it has been popular in England and North America over the past couple of decades. Other forms are Darin, Darrin, Darran, Darryn and Darien.

Darryl (m. and f.) From the Old English, "darling." Other forms are Darrell and Darrol.

David (m.) Biblical, from the boy David who slew the giant

Goliath, became king of Israel, and fathered Solomon. It derives from the Hebrew, "beloved." The name of the 6th-century patron saint of Wales, it is still immensely popular. It is shortened to Davey and Dave, and the Welsh form, Dafydd, is shortened to Dai and Taffy.

Davina (f.) The Scottish feminine form of David, it is also found in the forms Davinia and Davida.

Dawn (f.) An early 19th-century translation of the Latin name Aurora, "daybreak," which it superseded in popularity.

Dean (m.) Transferred use of the last name, from the Old English place name, meaning "valley." It was popularized by the singer Dean Martin (b.1917). The feminine form is Deanna.

Deborah (f.) From the Hebrew, "bee." The name of a prophetess in the Old Testament, and much favored by the Puritans of the 17th century, it has recently become popular again. A modern spelling is Debra, and short forms are Debbie, Debby and Deb.

Deirdre (f.) From the legendary Celtic heroine Deirdre of the Sorrows, who died of a broken heart after the man she jilted murdered her lover and his brothers. Deidrie and Deidra are variants.

Delia (f.) From Delos, birthplace of the goddess Artemis.

Delroy (m.) From the Old French, "belonging to the king." Like Leroy, it is a popular American name.

Delyth (f.) 20th-century Welsh name, meaning "pretty."

Denis (m.) From the Greek god of wine and revelry, Dionysos. It can also be spelled Dennis. The short forms are Den and Denny, and the feminine form is Denise (or Denyse or Denice). A related name from the same source is Dion, feminine form Dionne. Dionne Warwick, the singer, has made this last name well known.

Denzil (m.) Transferred use of a Cornish family name, from a place name.

Derek (m.) From the Old German name Theodoric,

"people's ruler." Variants are Derrick, Dery(c)k, Deric and Dirk (Dutch). Derry, Rick and Ricky are pet forms.

Dermot (m.) The anglicized version of the Irish name Diarmid, meaning "free of envy."

Desmond (m.) Transferred use of a last name, from the Irish, meaning "man from south of Munster." The shortened forms are Des and Desi.

Diana (f.) Latin name of the moon goddess, whose Greek name is Artemis. She was also goddess of hunting and protector of wild animals, and represented as being beautiful and chaste. The short form is Di, and variants are Diane and Dianne. The name has been made popular worldwide over the past decade by the present Princess of Wales.

Dick *see* Richard

Digby (m.) Transferred use of the last name, originally a place name in rural England, meaning "settlement by the dike."

Dilys (f.) Welsh, "steadfast," "true." The short form is Dilly.

Dinah (f.) Biblical: from the Hebrew, "judged." Also spelled Dina.

Dionne *see* Denis

Dolores (f.) Spanish, originally short for Maria de Dolores, Mary of the Sorrows. The pet forms, Lola and Lolita, are used as names in their own right.

Dominic (m.) From the Latin, "belonging to the Lord." The name of the founder of the Dominican monastic order and recently popular. Dominique is the feminine form.

Donald (m.) From the Gaelic, "world ruler," this name is particularly popular in Scotland. Donal is the Irish form, and the name is shortened to Don and Donny.

Donna (f.) From the Italian, "lady." Popular in North America.

Dora (f.) Originally a pet form of either Theodora or Dorothy, it became a popular name in its own right in the 19th century.

Doreen (f.) A variant of Dora, it began to be used at the beginning of the 20th century.

Doris (f.) Greek, "from the Dorian tribe." It was popular in the early decades of this century, but has since fallen out of fashion.

Dorothea, Dorothy (f.) From the Greek, meaning "gift of God." In the 16th century it was so popular that the pet name, Doll, was given to the little girl's toy. A Scottish word for a doll is Dorrity. Other pet names are Dolly, Dot, Dotty, Dodie, Dodo and Thea.

Dougal (m.) From the Gaelic, "dark stranger." Popular in the Highlands of Scotland, and also used as a lowland nickname for a Highlander.

Douglas (m.) Transferred use of the Scottish last name, from the Gaelic, "black stream." It can be abbreviated to Doug and Dougie.

Drusilla (f.) From a Roman family name.

Duane (m.) From the Celtic last name, "black." It was made famous by Duane Eddy in the 1950s, and the variants are Dwane and Dwayne.

Dudley (m.) From the English noble last name and place name, originally meaning "Dudda's wood clearing." It was made famous by comedian Dudley Moore, and is shortened to Dud.

Duncan (m.) From the Gaelic, "brown warrior." Borne by two kings of Scotland.

Dylan (m.) The name of a legendary Welsh hero and famous from the poet Dylan Thomas (1914-53).

E

Earl (m.) Mainly found in North America, this was originally a nickname from the aristocratic English title. A variant spelling is Erle.

Eartha (f.) From the Old English, "earth." Famous from the singer and actress Eartha Kitt.

Ebony (f.) From the black wood.

Edgar (m.) From the Old English, "happy spear," This was the name of a grandson of King Alfred the Great. It is now quite uncommon. The shortened forms are Ed and Eddie.

Edith (f.) From the Old English, "prosperous war." It was used throughout the Middle Ages and popular too in the late 19th century. The short forms are Eda and Edie.

Edmond, Edmund (m.) From the Old English, "happy protection." This name was borne by two kings of England and two saints. The Irish form is Eamon, and pet forms are Ned, Ted, Ed, Teddy and Eddie.

Edna (f.) An 18th-century variant of the Irish name Eithne or Aithne ("little fire"). It also appears in the Bible, where it comes from the Hebrew, "delight," as in the Garden of Eden. Eden is an unusual male variant.

Edward (m.) From the Old English, "guardian of riches." One of the most popular English names from the time of Edward the Confessor (c. 1002-66) to the present day. Queen Elizabeth II gave it to her youngest son. It shares pet names with Edmond.

Edwin (m.) From the Old English, "rich friend," it was very popular in Victorian times. It shares pet names with Edmond, and has the feminine form Edwina.

Eileen (f.) Of uncertain origin, possibly a Celtic substitute for Helen, and very popular in the late 19th century. Aileen is a variant.

Elaine (f.) A French form of Helen that sprang to popularity after the publication of Tennyson's *Idylls of the King* (1859).

Eleanor (f.) From a French form of Helen, it was introduced to England by Eleanor of Aquitaine, who married King Henry II in 1152. It can also be spelled Elinor, and has given rise to short forms and variations that have become names in their own right: Nell, Nellie, Ella, Ellie, Leonore and Leonora.

Eliot (m.) Transferred use of the last name, originally from the Hebrew Elias. It can also be spelled Elliott.

Elizabeth (f.) From the Hebrew, "oath of God." Made popular in the 16th century by Queen Elizabeth I of England, this is a name that has never been out of favor. It can also be spelled Elisabeth. Short forms and variants are Liz, Lizzie, Eliza, Elise, Babette (French), Bess, Bessie, Beth, Betty, Libby, Lisa, Lise, Lisette, Elsie and Elsa. In Scotland it becomes Elspeth.

Ella (f.) From the Old German, "all." Popular in the Middle Ages, it was revived in the 19th century.

Ellen (f.) A form of Helen.

Eloise (f.) She was the wife of the 12th-century scholar Abelard. Her guardian caused Abelard to be castrated, whereupon he became a monk and Eloise retreated to a nunnery. Heloise is a variant.

Elsa, Elsie *see* Elizabeth

Elton (m.) Transferred use of the last name, from the Old English place name, meaning "Ella's enclosure." Made popular by the singer Elton John.

Elvira (f.) Of obscure origin, this was a common name in the Middle Ages, but not used in English until the 19th century. It is best known from the title of the Swedish film *Elvira Madigan*.

Elvis (m.) There was a 6th-century Irish saint called Elvis, but the name remained virtually unknown until Elvis Presley (1935-78). It is often used in honor of the rock star, especially in America.

Emily (f.) This may come, like Amelia, from a Roman family name, or from the Old German meaning "hardworking." It was particularly popular in the 19th century, and is enjoying a revival today. Em, Emmy and Milly are the short forms, and Emilia (from the Italian) is a variant.

Emma (f.) From the Old German, "universal." Popular in England from the 11th century when Emma was Queen of Ethelred the Unready and later of King Canute. Always a favorite name, it has never been more popular than today. Em and Emmie are the pet forms.

Enoch (m.) Biblical: the son of Cain.

Eric (m.) From the Norse, "always rules." Rick and Ricky are short forms and Erica is the feminine. Erik and Erika are also found.

Erin (f.) From the Gaelic name for "Ireland." Enjoying recent popularity in North America.

Ernest (m.) From the Old German, "seriousness" or "vigor." The short forms are Ern and Ernie, and the feminine forms Ernestine and Ernestina.

Errol (m.) Transferred from the Scottish last name, this was originally a place name. Made famous by film star Errol Flynn (1909-59).

Esme (f.) From the Old French, "esteemed"; also related to Amy, "beloved."

Esther (f.) Biblical, deriving from the Persian word, "myrtle." A variant of the name is Hester, and the short forms are Etty and Hetty.

Euan (m.) A Gaelic name, meaning "born of the yew."

Eugene (m.) From the Greek, "well born," it is often shortened to Gene. Eugenia and Eugenie are the feminine forms.

Eunice (f.) From the Greek, "good victory." Used in the 17th century, it is also spelled Unice.

Eve (f.) Biblical: the first woman, created from Adam's rib,

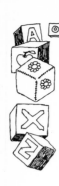

Evan

to whom he gave the name "mother of all living." Eva and Ava are variants and Evie and Evita are pet forms.

Evan (m.) Welsh for John ("God is gracious"), related to Ian, Euan and Ewan.

Evelyn (m. and f.) Transferred use of the last name, of uncertain origin.

F

Fabian (m.) From the Roman family name, originally meaning "bean-grower." The Roman general Fabius, who waged a delaying war of attrition on Hannibal without ever actually joining battle, inspired British socialists to name the Fabian Society after him in 1884.

Faith (f.) A 16th-century name that gained great popularity among the Puritans in the 17th century as one of the Christian virtues.

Fanny (f.) An abbreviation of Frances, used in its own right, but no longer popular.

Fay(e) (f.) From the Old English, "fairy." Famous from the Arthurian legends concerning King Arthur's mysterious sister Morgan le Fay.

Felicity (f.) From the Latin, "good fortune." A popular name among the Puritans of the 17th century, it has various short forms, including Fee and Fliss.

Felix (m.) From the Latin, "happy." Felicia and Felice are the feminine forms.

Fenella (f.) From the Gaelic, "white shoulders." Irish forms are Finola and Fionnuala, and shortened versions are Nella, Nola and Nuala.

Ferdinand (m.) From the Old German, "prepared for the journey," this name has always been popular in Spain, as Fernando and Ferdinando.

Fergus (m.) From the Gaelic, "chosen man." Popular in Scotland and Ireland, the shortened forms are Fergie and Gus.

Fern (f.) From the plant name, and increasingly popular.

Fiona (f.) From the Gaelic, 'white', 'fair'. The novelist William Sharp first used it in the 19th century as a pen name, Fiona Macleod. It is particularly popular in Scotland.

Flavia (f.) A Roman family name, originally meaning "golden haired."

Fleur (f.) From the French, "flower." It was popularized by the character in John Galsworthy's *The Forsyte Saga* (1922). Flower is also sometimes used.

Flora (f.) From the Latin, "flower," it was the name of the Roman goddess of flowers and the spring. It is particularly popular in Scotland because of Flora Macdonald, the heroine who helped Bonnie Prince Charlie escape to Skye in 1746.

Florence (f.) From the Latin, "blossoming." It enjoyed great popularity in the 19th century because of Florence Nightingale (1820-1910), who herself was named after the Italian city. The short forms are Flo, Florrie and Flossie. It is sometimes given to a boy in Ireland (shortened to Flurry).

Floyd (m.) From an English attempt to pronounce the Welsh last name Lloyd ("gray").

Frances (f.) From the Italian name Francesca, meaning "French." It became popular in England from the 15th century. Apart from Francesca, variants are Françoise and Francine, and short forms are Fran, Fanny, Francie and Frankie.

Francis (m.) From the same source as Frances, and meaning "Frenchman." Popular from the Middle Ages because of St. Francis of Assisi. Pet names are Frank and Frankie.

Frank (m.) From the Old German, meaning "of the tribe of the Franks." It is also short for Francis.

Franklin (m.) Transferred use of the last name, from the Middle English for "freeman."

Fraser (m.) Transferred use of the Scottish Highlander last name, originally meaning "curly-haired." It can also be spelled Frazer.

Freda (f.) This is the short form of names such as Winifred and Frederica, and has become a name in its own right. It can also be spelled Frieda, like the German form Friede, which means "peace."

Frederick (m.) From the Old German, "peaceful ruler." In Germany and Denmark it was much used by royal families. Also spelled Frederic, the short forms are Fred, Freddy and Freddie, and the feminine form is Frederica (Frederika).

Freya (f.) The name of the Norse goddess of love, beauty and fertility. The travel writer Freya Stark made this name well known.

G

Gabriel (m.) Biblical: the archangel who announced the news of Christ's forthcoming birth to Mary. Hebrew for "man of God." Nowadays the feminine forms Gabrielle and Gabriella, which can be shortened to Gaby, are more frequently found than the masculine form.

Gail (f.) The shortened form of Abigail ("father rejoiced"), which has existed in its own right only since the middle of this century. It is also spelled Gale and Gayle.

Gareth (m.) Welsh, of uncertain origin. Popular for its use in Arthurian legends and by the 19th-century poet Tennyson.

Garfield (m.) Transferred use of the last name, originally meaning "triangular field" or "field of spears."

Gary (m.) The short form of Gareth, Garfield and Gerard, Gary is also a name in its own right. It was made fashionable by the actor Gary Cooper (1901-61).

Gavin (m.) This comes from Sir Gawain, Knight of the Round Table in the Arthurian legends. Its original meaning was "hawk of May." It is very popular throughout the English-speaking world.

Gay(e) (f.) From the adjective, "lively," "happy." It also used to be a masculine name, but has fallen out of favor for both sexes since the 1960s, when "gay" came to mean "homosexual".

Gaynor (f.) Derives from the name of King Arthur's queen, Guinevere, which means "fair lady." Can be spelled Gayner and, as in Welsh, Gaenor.

Gemma (f.) From the Italian, "precious stone." Recently very popular, also in the spelling Jemma.

Genevieve (f.) A French name with Old German origins, meaning "woman of the race." St. Genevieve is patron saint of Paris, and the name is popular in France. It has been used in the English speaking world since the 19th century.

Geoffrey *see* Jeffrey

George (m.) From the Greek, "tiller of the soil," "farmer." St. George is patron saint of England, but not until 1714 did a George ascend the throne, and he was a German. The pet form is Georgie, and the feminine forms are Georgina, Georgine, Georgette, Georgiana or Georgia.

Geraint (m.) Welsh, from the Latin name Gerontius, which itself comes from the original Greek "old." The name was used by Tennyson in his *Idylls of the King* (1859).

Gerald (m.) From the Old German, meaning "rule by spear." Long popular in Ireland, the name was revived in the 19th century. It is sometimes spelled Jerrold or Jerald, and short forms are Gerry and Jerry. The feminine form is Geraldine.

Gerard (m.) From the Old German, "brave spear." Less common than Gerald, with which it shares short forms, it is favored mainly by Roman Catholics and can also be spelled Gerrard.

Germaine (f.) From the Latin, "a German." Well known because of Germaine Greer, the Australian feminist writer.

Gertrude (f.) From the Old German, "spear strength." Popular in the 19th century, it is not commonly found now, except in its short form Trudy. Gertie and Gert are other abbreviations.

Gilbert (m.) From the Old German, "bright pledge." Popular in Scotland and the north of England, it is shortened to Gil and Gilly.

Giles (m.) From the Greek, "young goat." The name was given to St. Giles, patron saint of beggars and cripples, because he wore a goatskin. He fled from Greece to France to escape the fame brought on by his miracles.

Gillian *see* Jill

Gina (f.) From Georgina, a short form that has established itself in its own right.

Gladys (f.) A Welsh name of uncertain origin, fashionable elsewhere in the late 19th century.

Glen(n) (m.) Celtic, "valley." Recently very popular, also in the form Glyn(n).

Glenda (f.) From the Welsh, "holy good." Well known since the fame of the actress Glenda Jackson.

Glenys (f.) From the Welsh, "holy." It can be spelled Glenis, Glennis and Glenice. A variant is Glynis.

Gloria (f.) From the Latin, "glory," this name first appeared in 1889 when George Bernard Shaw gave it to one of his characters in *You Never Can Tell*. Glory is the shortened form.

Glyn *see* Glen

Godfrey (m.) Old German, "God's peace." Common in medieval times but not often used now.

Gordon (m.) Transferred use of the Scottish last name,

from a place name. Taken up as a first name after the tragic death of General Gordon at Khartoum (1885).

Grace (f.) One of the popular virtue names of the 17th century, it was given a boost by Grace Darling, the lighthouse keeper's daughter who heroically saved sailors in a storm in 1838, and in the 20th century by the actress Grace Kelly (1928-82) who married Prince Rainier of Monaco. Gracie is the short form, as in the singer Gracie Fields.

Graham (m.) Transferred use of the Scottish last name, originally from Grantham, a place in Lincolnshire, Also spelled Grahame and Graeme. The short form is Gray.

Grant (m.) Transferred use of the last name, from the French, "big," "tall." It is often used in America in honour of General Grant, who was President from 1869 to 1876.

Gregory (m.) From the Greek, "watchful." This name was borne by 16 popes. The short form is Greg, and the Scottish Gregor.

Guinevere (f.) Welsh, "fair," "soft." Borne by King Arthur's wife, who fell in love with Sir Lancelot. The name gave rise to Jennifer, and Guenevere is an alternative form.

Gus *see* Angus, Augustus

Guy (m.) From the Old German, "wood" or "wide." It fell out of favor in the 17th century after Guy Fawkes and the Gunpowder Plot, but has recently become popular again in many places.

Gwendolyn (f.) From the Welsh, "white circle," this could also make reference to the moon goddess. It was the

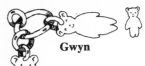

Gwyn

name of the fairy with whom King Arthur fell in love, and of the wife of the magician, Merlin. It can be spelled Gwendolen, and Gwen and Gwenda are short forms that have become independent names.

Gwyn (m.) Welsh, "fair." In England the name sometimes becomes Wyn. The feminine form, Gwyneth, means "blessed" or "happy," and can also be spelled Gwynneth.

H

Hamish (m.) The Gaelic form of James ("supplanter"), popular in Scotland.

Hannah (f.) Biblical: the mother of the prophet Samuel, it means "God has favored me." This name was loved in Victorian times and is enjoying a revival today.

Harold (m.) Old English, "ruler of the army." The name fell out of use after King Harold lost the Battle of Hastings in 1066, but became popular again in the 19th century. The short forms are Hal and Harry.

Harriet (f.) The feminine form of Henry, via Harry, and the short form of Henrietta. Ettie and Hattie are its own short forms. This name was very popular in the 18th and 19th centuries and is now enjoying a revival.

Harry (m.) The short form of Henry, used by the second son of the present Prince and Princess of Wales; also a name in its own right.

Harvey (m.) Transferred use of the last name, from the Breton, "worthy in battle."

Hayley (f.) Transferred use of the last name, from Old English, "hay field." Used only since it was made popular by the actress Hayley Mills in the 1960s.

Hazel (f.) One of a group of plant names adopted as first names at the end of the 19th century.

Heather (f.) A 19th-century plant name that enjoyed a revival in the 1950s.

Helen (f.) Greek, from the word for the sun. Helen of Troy was a legendary beauty, but the popularity of the name in Britain comes from the 4th-century St. Helena, thought to be the daughter of "Old King Cole," a prince of Colchester. In her eighties she visited the Holy Land, where it is said she found the true cross. Elena, Elaine and Ellen are other variants, and Lena is a short form of Helena. Helen is sometimes shortened to Nell.

Henrietta *see* Harriet

Henry (m.) From the Old German, "home ruler." The short forms are Harry and Hal, and Hank is used in North America.

Herbert (m.) From the Old German, "bright army." It became an aristocratic last name after the Norman Conquest, and was revived as a first name in the 19th century, when there was a fashion for using last names as first names. Bert, Herb and Herbie are the short forms.

Herman (m.) From the Old German for "army" and "man."

Hermione (f.) Greek, "daughter of Hermes." It was the name given to the daughter of Helen of Troy and Menelaus. It remains an unusual choice.

Hillary (f. and m.) This name used to be given to boys, though now it is more frequently a girl's name. It derives from the Latin for "cheerful."

Hilda (f.) Popular in the North of England because of the 7th century abbess of Whitby, this name comes from the Old German, "battle maid."

Holly (f.) After the plant, not used before the 20th century, but very popular since the 1960s.

Honor (f.) From the Latin, "reputation," "honour." One of the popular virtue names of the 17th century, its original form was Honoria.

39

Horace (m.) From the Roman family name Horatius. Famous from the poet Horace but rarely used nowadays. Horatio is a variant.

Howard (m.) English noble family name, from the Scandinavian, "high guardian." Alternatively, it could have denoted a medieval official, the hog warden or superintendent of pigs. Howie is the fashionable short form.

Hugh (m.) From the Old German, "heart," "mind" or "spirit." It appears in the Domesday Book and was made popular by the 12th-century bishop of Lincoln, St. Hugh, who was loved for his work among the poor. The Welsh form is Huw, and other variants are Hugo and Hubert, which means "bright heart." Short forms are Huey and Hughie.

Humphrey (m.) From the Old German, "giant peace." Never very popular, but famous because of the actor Humphrey Bogart and the jazz musician Humphrey Lyttleton.

Hywel (m.) Welsh, "eminent." It was common in the Middle Ages and is popular again in Wales today.

I

Ian (m.) Scottish version of John ("God is gracious"), now gaining popularity in the U.S. Iain is another spelling.

Ida (f.) From the Old German, "hard work." It became popular in the 19th century as the name given to the princess in Tennyson's poem and Gilbert and Sullivan's opera. Now it has dropped out of fashion again.

Idris (m.) Common in Wales, where it means "fiery lord."

The giant Idris, according to legend, was an astronomer and magician who lived on the mountain, Cader Idris.

Imogen (f.) First used by Shakespeare in *Cymbeline*, the name is thought to have been a printer's error for Innogen. The latter has Celtic origins and means "beloved child."

Iona (f.) From the Greek, "violet colored stone." Popular in Scotland, because of the Hebridean island of that name.

Irene (f.) From the Greek, "peace." Irene is one of the main characters in John Galsworthy's *The Forsyte Saga* (1922). The short form is Rene, pronounced with one or two syllables.

Iris (f.) Greek for "rainbow," this is the name of the goddess who used to cross a rainbow bridge to bring messages. The flower and the colored part of the eye were named after her for their brightness.

Irma (f.) Like Emma, this comes from the Old German, meaning "universal."

Isaac (m.) From the Hebrew, "laughter." Isaac was the son of Abraham and Sarah, conceived in her old age. It was most popular in the 17th century and can be abbreviated to Zak (from the spelling Izaak) or Ike.

Isabel (f.) Originally from the Spanish form of Elizabeth ("oath of God"), this name can also be spelled Isobel, and has the variants Isabella and Isabelle. Belle, Bella, Izzie and Isa are the short forms.

Isadora (f.) From the Greek, the feminine form of Isidore ("gift of Isis"), it can also be spelled Isidora. The name became well known because of the dancer Isadora Duncan (1878-1927).

Isla (f.) From the name of two rivers in Scotland, where it has become a popular girl's name.

Isolde (f.) The name of the beautiful Irish princess betrothed to King Mark of Cornwall, who drank a magic potion and fell in love with his envoy Tristram. Their tragic affair is charted in Wagner's opera *Tristan and Isolde*.

Ivor (m.) Of Scandinavian origin, its meaning is obscure; popular in Scotland and Wales, where it is spelled Ifor.

Ivy (f.) One of the plant names that came into popularity in the late 19th century.

J

Jack (m.) Originally used as a pet form of John ("God is gracious"), this has long been a name in its own right. In the Middle Ages it was so common that it became interchangeable with the word "man," as Jill was with "woman." The Scottish form, Jock, is still used to mean a Scotsman. Jake is a pet form of Jack, and that too has become an independent name.

Jackie *see* Jacqueline

Jacob (m.) Biblical: Jacob was the son of Isaac and Rebecca. He tricked his elder brother Esau out of his inheritance in exchange for a bowl of soup. He then tricked his father on his deathbed into blessing him instead of blessing Esau. The name is taken to mean "supplanter." It is related to James: Jacob comes from the Latin *Iacobus* and James from *Iacomus*. Jake is the short form.

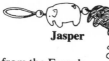

Jacqueline (f.) Like Jacquetta, this derives from the French form of Jacob and James (see above). It became especially popular in the 1960s because of Jacqueline Kennedy, later Jacqueline Onassis. There are various spellings, including Jackalyn and Jacquelyn, and the short forms are Jackie, Jacky and Jacqui.

Jake *see* Jack, Jacob

James (m.) The name of two of Christ's disciples. For its origins, see Jacob. It was used as a royal name from the 14th century on by the Scottish house of Stewart. The short forms are Jamie, Jim, Jimmy and Jimmie, and the Irish is Seamus.

Jane (f.) Like Joan and Jean, this was originally a feminine form of John ("God is gracious"). It can also be spelled Jayne, and pet forms are Janie and Janey. Janice and Janis have developed from it.

Janet (f.) Originally a diminutive of Jane, this name is particularly popular in Scotland. It has given rise to several other names: Jeanette, Janine, Janetta, and the pet forms Nettie, Netta and Jan, all used as names in their own right.

Janice *see* Jane

Jared (m.) From the Hebrew, meaning "servant" or "rose." This was very rare until the 1960s, when it found favor in North America and Australia. Variants are Jarrod and Jareth.

Jasmine (f.) From the flower name; the word has Persian origins. Other forms of this name include Jessamine, Jasmina, Yasmin and Yasmina.

Jason (m.) In ancient Greek legend, Jason was the leader of the Argonauts, who went in search of the Golden Fleece. It has become an extremely popular name in recent years.

Jasper (m.) Said by tradition to be one of the names of the Three Kings who visited Jesus at his birth (the other two were Balthazar and Melchior), it comes from the Persian, meaning "treasurer."

Jay (m.) From the bird, or an abbreviation of any names beginning with that letter.

Jean (f.) Along with Joan and Jane, this is derived from the French form of John ("God is gracious"). Particularly popular in Scotland. Jeannie is a pet form.

Jed (m.) The short form of Jedidiah, which means "beloved of God."

Jeffrey Old German in origin, this name could mean "peace of God" or "peace in the district." There were many distinguished bearers of the name in the Middle Ages, but then it fell out of popularity until the 19th century. It can also be spelled Geoffrey, and the short forms are Jeff and Geoff.

Jemima (f.) Biblical: Hebrew for "dove." Jemima was one of the daughters of Job (another was Kezia, a newly popular name). The short forms are Jem, Jemmy and Mima.

Jemma *see* Gemma

Jenna (f.) Recently invented variant of Jennifer.

Jennifer (f.) This was originally a Cornish form of Guinevere, wife of King Arthur. It has enjoyed enormous popularity in the 20th century. Short forms are Jen, Jenny and Jenni.

Jeremy (m.) Anglicized form of the Biblical name Jeremiah, "exalted by God." It is shortened to Jem and Jerry, which is used as a name in its own right.

Jerome (m.) From the ancient Greek, "holy name." Jerome was an early saint who translated the Bible into Latin. The name can be shortened to Jerry.

Jesse (m.) Popular in North America, this comes from the Hebrew, "gift." Jesse was the father of King David. Jess is the short form.

Jessica (f.) From the Hebrew, "God beholds," this name was introduced into English by Shakespeare in *The Merchant of Venice*. It is now very popular, and the short forms Jess and Jessie are names in their own right.

Jill From Julian, the name was so common in the Middle

Ages that it became the term for a woman, as Jack was for a man. It gave rise to the verb "to jilt," after which it fell out of favor. Gillian and Jillian are alternative spellings, and the short forms are Jill, Gill, Jilly and Gilly.

Jo (f. and m.) From Josephine or Joanna, this name sometimes combines with others, as in Mary Jo or Jo Anne. It can also be used for a boy, when it is usually spelled Joe, short for Joseph.

Joan (f.) Like Jean and Jane, it is one of the feminine forms of John. Popular from the Middle Ages, the name was given a boost by George Bernard Shaw's play *St. Joan* (1923), which tells the story of Joan of Arc (1412-31). The modern short form is Joni or Joanie.

Joanna (f.) From the Latin form of John. Its variants are Johanna and Joanne, and the short form is Jo.

Jocelyn (m. and f.) Like Joyce, a transferred use of the last name, this is derived from Norman French. It is now used more often for girls than for boys. The various spellings include Joscelin and Josslyn. Joss is the short form.

Joel (m.) Biblical, from the Hebrew, "Jehovah is the Lord." It has long been popular in America and is now finding increasing favor in Britain.

John (m.) From the Hebrew, "God is gracious." It has been one of the most common boy's names for centuries, and has given rise to many derivatives, including Jack, Jock, Ian, Iain, Ieuan, Evan, Sean and Shane. The short forms are Johnnie and Johnny.

Jonathan (m.) Biblical: the name of King David's friend, it

Joseph

comes from the Hebrew for "God has given." The short form is Jon, which has also become an independent name, and it can also be spelled Jonothon or Jonathon.

Joseph (m.) Biblical: the favorite son of Jacob, whose brothers sold him into slavery; also the husband of the Virgin Mary. It is a Hebrew word, meaning "God has added (to the family)." It was widely used in the 17th century, when the Puritans adopted many biblical names. The short forms are Jo, Joe, and Joss.

Josephine (f.) The feminine form of Joseph. The most famous bearer of the name has been Napoleon's Empress Josephine (1763-1814). Josie and Jo are the short forms.

Joshua (m.) From the Hebrew, "the Lord saves," it was the name of the Israelite leader who took over after the death of Moses and lead his people into the Promised Land. Josh is the short form.

Joy (f.) This name means what it says, and has been used since the 12th century. It came back into popularity in the first half of this century.

Joyce (f. and m.) This derives from the name of a 7th century Breton saint, Jodocus, via the French form Joisse. It is now rare as a boy's name, but enjoyed popularity as a girl's name in the first half of this century.

Jude (m.) From the Hebrew name Yehudi, this is the short form of Judas, the name of the apostle who betrayed Jesus, which explains why it has not enjoyed greater popularity. It came to public notice with Thomas Hardy's book *Jude the Obscure*, and more recently with the Beatles' song, *Hey Jude* (1968). Also a short form of the girl's name Judith.

Judith (f.) Biblical: from the Hebrew, meaning "Jewess," it was the name of Esau's wife and has always been particularly popular with Jewish parents. Judy (now a name in its own right), Judi and Jude are short forms. In Ireland the name has given rise to Siobhan.

Julia (f.) The feminine form of the Latin "Julius" meaning "hairy," it came to Britain from Italy in the 16th century, but was not in common use until the 18th and 19th centuries. Julie, the French short form, is now more common than Julia as a name in its own right. Other forms are Juliana and Juliet, famous as the lover of Romeo.

Julian (m.) From the Latin name Julius "hairy," this was borne by many saints and came to Britain in the 13th century. Older English forms are Julyan and Jolyon, which was used by John Galsworthy in *The Forsyte Saga* (1922). The French form, Jules, is occasionally used, both as a pet form and as an independent name.

Juliet *see* Julia

June (f.) The name of the month, and a 20th-century first name.

Justin (m.) From the Latin, "just," this name has been very popular over the last 20 years. The French feminine form, Justine, is also becoming known.

Karen (f.) A Scandinavian form of Katharine, this has been a popular choice in North America and more recently in Britain. Karin, Karon and Kara are variants, and these names are also found spelled with a "C."

Karl (m.) The German form of Charles ("man"). Like the feminine, Karla, it can be spelled with a "C."

Kate (f.) Originally a diminutive of Katharine. Popular since the Middle Ages, it was used by Shakespeare, and is a name in its own right, with the short forms Katy or Katie.

Katharine (f.) From the Greek, "pure," this name was brought to Britain by the Crusaders in the 12th century

47

with the legend of St. Katharine of Alexandria, who was martyred for her faith. The alternative spelling is Catherine, and the short forms are Kate, Kitty, Katie, Cathy and Kay. Variants are Kathleen (Irish), Catriona (Scottish) and Kathryn; Katrina and Caitlin are derivatives.

Kay(e) (f.) A short form of Katharine or any other name beginning with "K," and a name in its own right for the past 100 years.

Keith (m.) Transferred use of the last name, from a Scottish place name, originally meaning "wood."

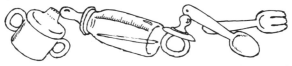

Kelly (f. and m.) An Irish last name, meaning "warrior," it has recently been used as a first name, more often for girls than boys.

Kenneth (m.) From the Gaelic, "handsome," this name has been popular in Scotland since Kenneth MacAlpine became the first king of Scotland in the 9th century. Short forms are Ken and Kenny.

Kent (m.) From the English county, and popular recently in North America.

Kenton (m.) Transferred use of the last name, meaning "royal enclosure."

Kerry (f. and m.) From the Irish county, and originally used in Australia as a boy's name, though now more common, in the U.S. too, for girls.

Kevin (m.) From the Irish, "handsome at birth." St. Kevin was a 6th-century hermit. It is now a very popular name throughout the English-speaking world. The short form is Kev.

Kieran (m.) From the Irish, "dark-haired." Popular in the past two decades, it can also be spelled Keiran and Kieron.

Kim (m. and f.) Often short for Kimberley, this used always to be a boy's name, but is now given almost exclusively to girls and is a name in its own right. It came to public attention in 1901 with Rudyard Kipling's novel *Kim*, in which the hero bore the name as a shortened form of Kimball.

Kimberley (f. and m.) The name of a mining town in South Africa, and no doubt popular as a name because of its association with diamonds. Sometimes used for boys, it is more often a girl's name now, particularly in North America.

Kirsty (f.) The Scottish form of Christine ("Christian"), it has become popular alongside its Scandinavian form Kirsten.

Kyle (m.) Transferred use of the Scottish last name, it means "a narrow strip of land or water."

Kylie (f.) An Australian girl's name meaning "boomerang," now popular all over the English-speaking world.

Lana *see* Alan

Lance (m.) From the Old German word for "land" and also short for Lancelot, the knight of the Arthurian legends.

Lara (f.) Russian and Italian, short for Larissa ("laughing"). It became popular because of the heroine in the film *Dr. Zhivago* (1965).

Laura (f.) Like Laurence, this is derived from the Latin for "laurel," the leaves of which formed a wreath given to conquerors and poets. Laura was also the name of the mistress of the 14th-century Italian poet Petrarch. The name has many derivatives, including Loretta, Lauren,

Laurence

Laurel itself and the variant Lorel; Laurissa, Laureen, and Lolly. Lol and Laurie are pet forms.

Laurence (m.) From the Latin, "a man from Laurentum" ("city of laurels"). It can also be spelled Lawrence and the short forms are Laurie, Lawrie and Larry (now a name in its own right).

Lavinia (f.) A classical Roman name popular during the Renaissance and briefly in the 18th century. It was said to be the name of the wife of Aeneas.

Leah (f.) The name means "languid" in Hebrew. Leah was the elder sister of Rachel, for whose hand Jacob labored for seven years. He was then tricked into marrying Leah, though Rachel was given to him afterwards, in return for another seven years' labor. It can also be spelled Lea and Lia.

Leanna (f.) From the French, "climbing vine." It can also be spelled Liana, Leana or Leanne, and another form is Leigh Anne.

Lee, Leigh, Lea (m. and f.) this name originally meant "meadow" in Old English. It first became popular in North America, but is now widely used all over the English-speaking world.

Leila (f.) A Persian name, meaning "dark-haired," it became fashionable in the early 19th century when used by Byron for two of his heroines.

Lena *see* Helen

Leo (m.) Latin, "lion." The name of 6 emperors and 13 popes. Leon is an alternative form and Leonie and Leona are the feminine forms.

Leonard (m.) From the Old German, meaning "brave lion." St. Leonhard was a 6th-century hermit who

50

became patron saint of prisoners. Len and Lenny or Lennie are the short forms.

Leonora, Lenore, Leonore (f.) These names all derive from Eleanor (and so from Helen) and were first used in the 19th century. Nora is a short form.

Leroy (m.) From the Old French, "the king."

Lesley, Leslie (f. and m.) Transferred use of the Scottish last name. The first spelling used to be exclusively for girls and the second for boys, but now the two are interchangeable.

Lester (m.) Transferred use of the last name, which comes from the English place name Leicester.

Lettice (f.) A variant of the name Laetitia, or Letitia, from the Latin, "gladness." Lettie and Letty are the short forms.

Lewis (m.) From the Old German, "famous warrior," this name is related to Ludovic and Clovis. The French form, also used, is Louis. The short forms are Lou or Lew and Louie.

Liam (m.) The Irish equivalent of William (from Old German "resolution" and "helmet"), this is now also popular outside Ireland.

Libby *see* Elizabeth

Lillian (f.) This has been in use since the 16th century and could have derived from Elizabeth ("oath of God"). It is not connected with Lily, which is a 19th-century name. It can also be spelled Lilian, and has the short form Lil.

Lily (f.) A 19th-century flower name. The short form is Lil.

Linda (f.) This is a 19th-century name deriving from the Old German word for a serpent, the embodiment of wisdom and suppleness. The Spanish word *linda* means "pretty." The name can also be the short form of Belinda. The alternative spelling is Lynda, and short forms are Lindie, Lyn and Lynne, which are independent names.

Lindsay (f. and m.) Transferred use of the Scottish last name, originally from a place name in rural England.

Also spelled Lindsey or Linsey, this is now a more common girl's name than a boy's name.

Lionel (m.) The French diminutive of Leon, "little lion."

Lisa *see* Elizabeth

Llewellyn (m.) From the Welsh, "like a lion." The short forms are Lew and Lyn.

Lloyd (m.) This comes from the Welsh last name meaning "gray." Floyd is an American name that has derived from it because of the difficulty of pronouncing the Welsh double "l."

Lois (f.) A name of uncertain derivation, it occurs in the New Testament, where St. Paul wrote two epistles to Timothy, who has a grandmother called Lois.

Loretta *see* Laura

Lorna (f.) Coined by R.D. Blackmore in his novel *Lorna Doone* (1869). Lorne is the masculine form.

Lorraine (f.) Means "from the province of Lorraine in France," which originally was called "Lothar's place." A very popular name in North America and Britain, it can also be spelled Lorayne and Loraine.

Louis *see* Lewis

Louise (f.) The feminine form of Louis and Lewis, "famous in war." Louisa is also popular. Lou and Lulu are the short forms.

Lucy (f.) From the Latin for "light," the name was once given to girls born at dawn. The goddess Lucina was the patroness of childbirth. Luce is an older form and the Italian Lucia is another variant that is again being used in the U.S. Lucinda, with its short form Cindy, is a poetic alternative, and others are Lucasta, Lucette, Lucie and Lucille. The masculine forms, less well known, are

Lucien and Lucian. Lucy was extremely popular in Victorian times and is back in fashion again today.

Luke (m.) From the Greek, meaning "man from Lucania," Luke was the writer of the third gospel. It has recently become very popular.

Luther (m.) From the Old German, "famous warrior." Martin Luther was the 16th-century religious reformer, after whom the 20th-century civil rights campaigner Martin Luther King (1929-68) was named.

Lydia (f.) Means "woman from Lydia," in Asia Minor. It was not used in Britain before the 17th century.

Lynda *see* Linda

Lynn (f.) This developed from the short form of Linda, or from the short form of Carolyn. It is now an independent name.

M

Mabel (f.) Originally the short form of Amabel, "lovable." It was popular from the 12th to the 15th century, and revived again in the 19th, since when it has fallen out of use.

Madeleine (f.) From the French for Mary Magdalene, who came from Magdala on the Sea of Galilee. It can also be spelled Madeline and Madaleine and has the short forms Maddy and Madge, which it shares with Margaret.

Madonna (f.) From the Italian, "my lady," and usually applied to the Virgin Mary, this name has now been taken up by Italian-Americans particularly since the fame of the pop star Madonna (b.1959).

Mae *see* May

Maeve (f.) From the Celtic, meaning "intoxicating," this was the name of a legendary Irish warrior queen.

Maggie *see* Margaret

Magnus (m.) From the Latin, "great," this name may stem from the Emperor Charlemagne, who was called Carolus Magnus (Charles the Great). In Ireland the name has become Manus, and formed the last name, McManus.

Maisie (f.) Scottish form of Margaret ("pearl") and a name in its own right, made famous by Henry James's novella *What Maisie Knew* (1897).

Malcolm (m.) From the Gaelic, "servant of St. Columba." A very popular name in Scotland, where four kings bore this name. The short form is Mal.

Mamie (f.) An American pet form of Mary, also shortened to Mame.

Mandy (f.) Pet form of Amanda ("worthy to be loved"), now given in its own right.

Marcia (f.) The feminine form of the Latin Marcius, a Roman family name, possibly from the god Mars. Variants include Marsha, Marcella, Marcellina, Marcelle and Marcine. Marcie and Marcy are short forms.

Marcus (m.) A Roman family name, possibly from the god of war, Mars. It has given rise to the name Mark, popular because of the apostle of that name. The Venetians built St. Mark's cathedral in his honor and also put his symbol on their coins, which came to be known as "marks." The French forms Marc and Marcel are also found.

Margaret (f.) Comes from the Greek, "pearl." It has been immensely popular in Scotland since the 11th century, when St. Margaret became wife of King Malcolm III. There was a revival of the name in England in the 19th century and it is popular in the U.S. There are many variations and pet names, including Margot, Marguerite, Margaretta, Margarita, Madge, Meg, Maggie, Megan, Greta, Rita, Peg and Peggy.

Margery (f.) This developed from Marguerite (see above), and can also be spelled Marjorie. Madge and Marge are short forms.

Margot *see* Margaret

Maria, Marie *see* Mary

Marian (f.) Originally a diminutive form of Mary, this was established as a separate name by the Middle Ages. It can be spelled Marion. Marianne and Marianna come from the compound Mary Ann. Marianna and Annemarie are variations.

Marigold (f.) One of a group of flower names adopted in the late 19th century.

Marilyn (f.) From the combination of Mary and Lynne, this name was given glamor by the actress Marilyn Monroe (1926-62). It can also be spelled Maralyn and Marilene.

Marina (f.) From the Latin, meaning "of the sea." It has been used since the 14th century, but received a boost in popularity when it was introduced into the British royal family by the marriage of Princess Marina of Greece to Prince George in 1934.

Marisa *see* Mary

Marjorie *see* Margery

Mark *see* Marcus

Marlene (f.) This derives from Mary Magdalene and was introduced to the English-speaking world from the German by actress Marlene Dietrich (1901-92) and the 1940s song *Lili Marlene*. Marlena is another form.

Marlon (m.) Of unknown origins, this name has become famous because of film actor Marlon Brando (b.1924). It was also borne by his father.

Martha (f.) From the Aramaic, "lady." Biblical: the name of the sister of Lazarus and Mary of Bethany, who complained about the burden of housework. The short forms, Marti and Marty, are now more fashionable.

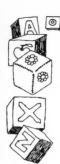

Martin

Martin (m.) Like Marcus and Mark, this is derived from the Roman god of war, Mars. It was the name of a 4th-century saint and of the Protestant reformer Martin Luther. A very popular name, it can also be spelled Martyn, and the short forms are Mart and Marty. Martina is the feminine form, borne by the tennis champion Martina Navratilova.

Marvin (m.) From the Welsh "sea hill," it is a variant of Merlin, King Arthur's magician. It can also be spelled Marvyn and Mervin.

Mary (f.) The original meaning of this name is thought to be "wished-for child." The earliest form of the name in the Bible was Miriam. It has been used, in many forms, in honor of the Virgin Mary, but was held to be too sacred for general use before the 12th century. Among the many variants are Maria, Marie, Moira and Maire (Irish), Mairi, Marietta, Mariella, Marisa, Mariel and Maire. Pet forms include Molly, Polly, Mimi, Minnie, Mamie and May or Mae.

Matilda (f.) From the Old German, "mighty battle maid." Popular in the Middle Ages, the name enjoyed a revival in the 18th century. Mattie and Tilly are short forms.

Matthew (m.) From the Hebrew, "gift of God." The name of one of the apostles, it was very popular in the Middle Ages and is enjoying a great revival today. Matt is the short form.

Maud (f.) A medieval variant of Matilda, the name was revived in the 19th century when Tennyson's poem of that name brought it into the public eye. It is also spelled Maude, and Maudie is the pet form.

Maureen (f.) A variant of Maire, the Irish form of Mary. The short form is Mo.

Maurice (m.) From the Latin Mauritius, "Moor." Maurice is the French form, which has superseded the English Morris in popularity. Morrie, Moss and Mo are the short forms.

Mavis (f.) The old word for a "songthrush," this was first used as a given name by Marie Corelli in her novel *The Sorrows of Satan* (1895).

Maximilian (m.) From the Latin, "greatest." Now popular in its short form Max, this name spread to Britain and America from Germany. Maxim and Maxwell are variants. Maxi is a pet form.

Maxine (f.) The feminine form of Max, it came into use this century.

May (f.) Originally a short form of Margaret or Mary, it is now a name in its own right, associated with the springtime month. It can also be spelled Mae and Mai. Maia and Maya are alternatives.

Megan (f.) Welsh, from Meg, the pet form of Margaret ("pearl").

Melanie (f.) From the Greek, "dark complexioned." It was introduced to England from France in the 17th century and became very popular during the 20th century after it was given to one of the heroines in the novel *Gone With The Wind* (1936).

Melissa (f.) From the Greek, "bee." First popular in the 17th century, it has enjoyed a huge revival recently, both in Britain and in America.

Melody (f.) A musical name that has recently become popular.

Melvin (m.) Probably from the Celtic, "chief." It can also be spelled Melvyn and is shortened to Mel.

Meredith (f. and m.) Transferred use of the Welsh last name, meaning "great chief." The female short form is Merry, which is also the short form of the virtue name, Mercy.

Meriel

Meriel (f.) From the Celtic, "bright as the sea," and a variant of Muriel.

Merle (f.) From the French, "blackbird," this name was adopted in the 19th century. Another form is Meryl, as in the actress Meryl Streep, and the masculine forms are Merrill, Myre and Merryl.

Mervyn *see* Marvin.

Mia (f.) From the Italian, "mine," this name is best known from the actress Mia Farrow (b.1945).

Michael (m.) From the Hebrew, this means "who is like God" and was borne in the Bible by one of the archangels, Michael, patron saint of soldiers. In Ireland the name is so popular that the short form, Mick, is a nickname for an Irishman. Mike, Mikey and Mickey are the other short forms. Michelle (short form Shelly) and Michaela are the girls' names.

Michelle (f.) From Michael, see above, this French feminine form is now very popular in England and the U.S., probably largely because of the Beatles' 1960s song of that name.

Mildred (f.) From the Old English, "gentle defense," this was popular in the 19th century. Milly and Millie are the short forms.

Miles (m.) Could come from the Old German, "beloved," or from the Latin, "soldier." It was popular in the Middle Ages, also in the forms Milo and Milon, and has enjoyed a revival in the 19th and 20th centuries. Myles is an alternative spelling.

Millicent (f.) From the Old German, meaning "labor" and "strength," this was introduced via the French name Melisande, and was fashionable in Victorian times. It shares the short forms Millie and Milly with Mildred.

Milton (m.) From the last name, originally a place name, meaning "mill enclosure." It gained fame from the poet, John Milton (1608-74).

Mimi *see* Mary

Miranda (f.) Invented by Shakespeare for the heroine in

The Tempest, it comes from the Latin for "worthy to be admired." Most popular in the 20th century, it shares its pet form, Mandy, with Amanda.

Miriam (f.) The earliest recorded form of Mary ("wished-for child"), this name has long been popular with Jewish families. The sister of Moses and Aaron was called Miriam. Short forms can be Mim, Minnie and Mitzi.

Mitchell (m.) Transferred use of the last name, derived in turn from the given name Michael. Popular in America, this can be shortened to Mitch.

Moira (f.) A variant of Maire, the Irish form of Mary ("wished-for child"). The alternative forms are Moyra and Maura.

Molly (f.) A pet form of Mary ("wished-for child"), and long a name in its own right.

Monica (f.) The name is of uncertain origin. St. Monica was the mother of St. Augustine. The French form Monique and the short form Mona are also found.

Montagu(e) (m.) Comes from the French, meaning "pointed mountain." This name was brought to England with William the Conqueror, and was adopted along with many other aristocratic last names in the 19th century. It shares the short form Monty with Montgomery.

Montgomery (m.) From the Old French, "mountain of the powerful man." Mainly a last name, it was given a boost as a first name by the actor Montgomery Clift (1920-66). The short form is Monty.

Morag (f.) A Scottish name from the Gaelic, "great."

Morgan (m. and f.) From the Old Celtic, "sea bright." King Arthur's step-sister was called Morgan le Fay.

Morna

Morna (f.) From the Gaelic, "beloved." A variant is Myrna.

Mortimer (m.) Transferred use of the last name, from the French place name, originally meaning "dead sea." Morty and Mort are the short forms.

Morven (f.) An Irish name, meaning "tall peak."

Morwenna (f.) A Welsh name, meaning "maiden."

Muriel (f.) From the Celtic, "sea bright," this name came to Britain at the time of the Norman Conquest. Its popularity was revived in the 19th century, but now the variant Meriel is more favored.

Murray (m.) A Celtic clan name, meaning "sea," and probably taken from the Moray Firth. It can also be spelled Moray, and Murry is the Irish form.

Myfanwy (f.) Welsh, meaning "my rare one." The short forms are Myf, Myfi and Fanny.

Myra (f.) A literary invention of the 17th century that was not used outside the world of books until the 19th century.

Myron (m.) From the Greek for the fragrant resin, myrrh.

Myrtle (f.) From the plant which to the ancient Greeks was a symbol of victory, this name was a 19th-century introduction. Myrtilla is also sometimes found.

N

Nadia (f.) Like Nadine, this comes from the Russian, meaning "hope." Both names have been popular in the 20th century. Nada and Nadya are other forms.

Nan, Nanette *see* Ann

Nancy (f.) One of the pet forms of Ann ("grace"), this name has been used in its own right for 200 years.

Neville

Naomi (f.) From the Hebrew, "pleasant." In the Bible, Naomi was the mother-in-law of Ruth. It was favored in the 17th century by the Puritans and is currently enjoying something of a revival.

Narelle (f.) An Australian girl's name.

Natalie (f.) From the Russian, Natalya, this name came to the U.S. via the Ballet Russe in the early 20th century. Its original meaning is "the Lord's birthday." Now very popular, it is also found in the form Nathalie.

Natasha (f.) This is the Russian pet form of Natalie. It is sometimes shortened to Tasha or Nettie. It is popular today.

Nathan (m.) From the Hebrew, "gift." The name of a prophet who had the courage to stand up to King David. An increasingly popular choice in the 20th century.

Nathaniel (m.) Another Biblical name that is enjoying a revival, especially in America. It means, in Hebrew, "gift of God," and is often shortened to Nat.

Ned see Edmund, Edward

Neil (m.) From the Gaelic, Niall, it may mean "cloud" or "champion." An enormously popular name in Scotland and Ireland, it is now widely used throughout the English-speaking world. Other spellings are Neill and Neal. Niall is a common spelling in Ireland and Scotland.

Nell (f.) A pet form of Eleanor, Helen and Ellen, this is also a name in its own right. Nelly and Nellie are pet forms.

Nelson (m.) Transferred use of the last name, and given in honor of the British Lord Horatio Nelson (1758-1805).

Nerys (f.) Welsh, meaning "lady." This name has become known through the actress Nerys Hughes.

Nesta (f.) A Welsh name, a pet form of Agnes ("pure"), along with Nessa and Nessie (which can also be short forms of Vanessa).

Neville (m.) Transferred use of the French last name, meaning "new town." First used as a given name in the 17th century and now very popular.

Niall

Niall *see* Neil

Nicholas (m.) From the Greek, "victory to the people." Very popular in the Middle Ages because of St. Nicholas, patron saint of children and sailors, who has survived in legend as Santa Claus. Now one of the most popular boys' names, it can be shortened to Nick, Nicky and Nico. Nicol is another form.

Nicola, Nicolette (f.) The feminine forms of Nicholas. Nicole, Nicky, Nikki and Nichola are other related names.

Nigel (m.) This name is related to Neil and derives from the Irish word for "champion." Nigel, along with the forms Nigell and Nygell, was popular in the Middle Ages, and remains in use today. The short form is Nige.

Nina (f.) Russian, short for Annina, Antonina and similar names, and established as a name in its own right for about a hundred years.

Nita (f.) Short for Anita and other names that end with these syllables.

Noël (m.) From the French, "Christmas." Girls are given the form Noëlle or Noële.

Nolan (m.) Transferred use of the Irish last name, meaning "champion."

Nona (f.) From the Latin, "ninth," this used to be given to the ninth-born child, if it was a girl. In these days of smaller families it is not so much used.

Nora(h) (f.) An Irish abbreviation of the name Honora, meaning "honor." Another variant is Noreen. It is popular with Irish parents.

Norma (f.) Of disputed origin, but could be from the Latin, "rule." It was not popular until Bellini's opera of that name (1831) brought it to public notice. It was much used earlier this century in Britain and America.

Norman (m.) From the Old German, "Norseman." It was known in Britain before the Norman Conquest and has long been popular in Scotland. Norrie and Norm are the pet forms.

62

O

Octavia (f.) From the Latin, "eighth," it used to be given to the eighth child if it was a girl, or the eighth girl. However families are smaller nowadays.

Odette (f.) French, but of Germanic origin, meaning "rich," this name remains unusual in America and Britain.

Olaf (m.) From the Old Norse, meaning "ancestor" and "heir." It is quite popular in America, especially among families of Scandinavian descent.

Olga (f.) Russian, originally meaning "holy." Helga is the Scandinavian form. The name was first used in England in the 19th century.

Olive *see* Olivia

Oliver (m.) From the French, "olive tree"; it may be also connected to Olaf (see above). It was a popular name until the 17th century, but after Oliver Cromwell it lost favor for a couple of hundred years. It is enjoying a revival today. Ol, Ollie, Noll and Nolly are the pet forms.

Olivia (f.) From the Latin, "olive." Olive has been used as a given name since the 19th century, when it came into popularity with a host of other plant names, probably partly because an olive branch symbolizes peace. Olivia was first used by Shakespeare in *Twelfth Night* and is the more popular form today.

Olwen (f.) From the Welsh, "white footprint." In Arthurian legend the giant's daughter Olwyn was given her name because white clover sprang up wherever she walked. The name spread from Wales and is sometimes spelled Olwyn.

Omar (m.) A biblical name meaning "eloquent" used by the Puritans in the 17th century, it appears occasionally in America, and was made more popular by the actor Omar Sharif.

Oona, Oonagh *see* Una

Ophelia

Ophelia (f.) From the Greek, "help," this name was chosen by Shakespeare for the girl who falls in love with Hamlet, goes mad and drowns herself. It has been quite popular since the 19th century and is still occasionally used today.

Oriana (f.) From the Latin for "dawn." The French name Oriane is sometimes found also. Oriana was used by madrigal writers in the 16th century as a name for Queen Elizabeth I.

Orlando (m.) The name given to the hero in Shakespeare's *As You Like It*. It gained some popularity earlier this century when Virginia Woolf wrote a novel of that name.

Orson (m.) From the Latin, "bear," this name was made famous by the actor Orson Welles (1915-85).

Orville (m.) From the French, meaning "gold town," this name was famously borne by Orville Wright, the pioneer aviator (1871-1948).

Osbert (m.) From the Old English, "bright god." It was a popular name in the 19th century, but has now fallen out of favor. Osbert Sitwell, the writer, and Osbert Lancaster, the cartoonist, are two famous bearers of the name this century.

Oscar (m.) From the Old English, "god spear," it was the name of Ossian's son in James Macpherson's poems of the 1760s. Napoleon gave the name to his godson in honor of this fictional hero; he later became King of Sweden. The name became widely popular all over Europe, only to fall out of use with the imprisonment of the writer Oscar Wilde (1854-1900).

Oswald (m.) From the Old English, "god power," this was the name of two saints. It fell from popularity after the Middle Ages and enjoyed a brief revival in the 19th century.

Otis (m.) Transferred use of the last name. It is used in the U.S. in honor of the singer Otis Redding (1941-67).

Otto (m.) Otto the Great (912-73) was the founder of the

Holy Roman Empire, and the name means "riches" in Old German. It was often used by the royal houses of Germany and Austria.

Owen (m.) One of the most popular boys' names in Wales, now used also in England and the U.S., it is of uncertain origin but may be related to Eugene, and mean "well born." Owen Glendower, the Welsh independence fighter of the 15th century, was one famous bearer of the name.

Oz (m.) Short for Osbert and Oswald, this is sometimes given as a name in its own right. It has the pet forms Ozzy and Ozzie.

P

Paddy (m.) This is a pet form of Patrick, a name so common in Ireland that in England Paddy has become the nickname for all Irishmen.

Paige (f.) A modern American name, a transferred use of the last name.

Pamela (f.) From the Greek, "all honey," this name was coined by the Elizabethan poet Sir Philip Sidney and also used by Samuel Richardson in his novel of that name (1740). Pamella is a modern spelling which reflects the original pronunciation, with the stress on the second syllable. Pam and Pammie are short forms.

Pandora (f.) In Greek mythology, Pandora was the first woman on Earth, put there as the scourge of men, as a revenge for their theft of fire from the gods. She was given a box which she was forbidden to open, but curiosity overcame her; she lifted the lid, and every imaginable type of ill escaped. The only thing left inside the box was hope. The ironic meaning of the name is "all gifts."

Pansy (f.) One of the 19th-century flower names, it has not been popular since the word has come to mean a homosexual. The word pansy comes from the French *pensée*, thought.

Pascal (m.) From the Latin, "Easter," it is a French name given in honor of the Resurrection or to children born at that time of year. The feminine form is Pascale, and the name has been used since the 1960s.

Pat *see* Patricia, Patrick

Patience (f.) One of the virtue names adopted by the Puritans in the 17th century, this is not often found today. Pat is the short form.

Patricia (f.) The feminine form of Patrick, this comes from the Latin, "nobleman." It became popular at the turn of the century when Queen Victoria's granddaughter was named Princess Patricia of Connaught. Short forms are Trish, Tricia, Pat, Pattie, Patsy and Paddy.

Patrick (m.) From the Latin, "nobleman." St. Patrick is the patron saint of Ireland, who spent his life converting the Irish to Christianity. The Irish thought his name too holy to use before the 17th century, but now it is so common that the short form, Paddy, has come to be the English nickname for an Irishman. Patrick is popular throughout the English-speaking world and can also be abbreviated to Pat.

Patsy (f.) Though sometimes given as the short form of Patrick in Ireland, elsewhere it is exclusively a feminine name. In the U.S. it is a slang word meaning "dupe," and in Australia it means "homosexual," but it is nevertheless a popular girl's name in both countries. It is sometimes used in combination with other names, as in Patsy Ann.

Paul (m.) From the Latin, "small." Saul of Tarsus took this name on his conversion on the road to Damascus. The name was not used widely until this century, when it has become very popular.

Paula, Paulette, Pauline (f.) These are the feminine forms of Paul. Pauline was most popular earlier on this century, but has given way latterly to Paula. A pet form of all three names is Polly, and this is often used independently.

Pearl (f.) This is one of a group of 19th-century jewel names. It was also used as a pet name for Margaret, which derives from the Greek for "pearl." It has fallen out of favor.

Peg, Peggy *see* Margaret

Penelope (f.) Of uncertain origin, but it may come from the Greek, "weaver." It was the name of the mythical hero Odysseus's wife and has been used in Britain since the 16th century. Pen and Penny are the short forms.

Penny *see* Penelope

Percival (m.) Transferred use of the last name, from a place name in Normandy, meaning "pierce the valley." In Arthurian legend Perceval was the only knight destined to find the Holy Grail, because of his purity of character. Perceval is a variant; Percy is the short form.

Percy (m.) Transferred use of the aristocratic Norman French last name. The poet Percy Bysshe Shelley (1792-1822) was so named because he was distantly descended from the Percy family, and the name was thereafter given in honor of him, though it has now fallen out of favor.

Peregrine (m.) From the Latin, "foreigner" or "traveler," it gave rise to the word pilgrim. It has been used frequently since the 13th century, and the short form is Perry.

Perry

Perry (m.) The short form of Peregrine, this also evolved independently from the last name, which means "someone who lives by a pear tree."

Peter (m.) From the Greek, "rock." Peter was the chief of Christ's apostles and the founder of the Church of Rome. The name is first recorded in England in the Domesday Book, and it was popular until the Reformation, when its association with the papacy put it out of favor. It began to be used widely again when James Barrie's *Peter Pan* was published in 1904. The short form is Pete, and Peta and Petra are the feminine forms.

Petula (f.) From the Latin, "seeker," and made famous by the singer Petula Clarke. The short form is Pet.

Philip (m.) From the Greek, "lover of horses." Philip of Macedon was the father of Alexander the Great, and several early saints bore the name. It fell out of favor in the reign of Queen Elizabeth I, when King Philip of Spain was her enemy, but has been very popular since, partly because of Prince Philip, the present Duke of Edinburgh. It can also be spelled Phillip, and the short forms are Phil, Flip and Pip.

Philippa (f.) This name evolved through a clerical distiction between the sexes. In the Middle Ages, both men and women called Philip, and an "a" was added on paper to mark the female bearers of the name. It has been popular, along with its pet form Pippa, since the 19th century.

Phoebe (f.) Means "bright" and was one of the names the ancient Greeks bestowed on the goddess of the moon and of hunting. She was the sister of Apollo. It was popular in Victorian times and is enjoying a modest revival today.

Phyllis (f.) From the Greek, "leafy." It was the name of a mythical girl who died of love and was turned into an almond tree. The pet form is Phil, and the name can also be spelled Phillis.

Piers (m.) This is the Middle English form of Peter ("rock"), as in the medieval poem *Piers Plowman*. In the 18th century it was transformed into Pierce, but this has generally died out, and Piers is becoming popular again.

Pippa *see* Philippa

Polly *see* Pauline, Mary

Poppy (f.) One of a group of flower names introduced in the 19th century, it was particularly popular in the 1920s.

Portia (f.) From the Roman family name, which derives from the Latin for "pig." Shakespeare gave it to his heroine in *The Merchant of Venice*, which boosted its popularity.

Primrose (f.) One of the 19th-century flower names, it comes from the Latin, "first rose."

Priscilla (f.) From the Latin word, "ancient," it was the name of a woman of Corinth, with whom St. Paul stayed on his travels. Priscilla was popular among the Puritans of the 17th century, and later with the Victorians. Prissy is one short form, but the other, more popular abbreviation is Cilla, which became popular in the late 1960s.

Prudence (f.) This appears in Chaucer's 14th-century poems and was one of the abstract virtue names favored in the 17th century by the Puritans. Unlike Temperance, Silence and other fun-denying names, Prudence has survived and remains well liked. The short forms are Pru and Prue.

Prunella (f.) This is the diminutive of the Latin word for "plum," and means "plum-colored" in French.

69

Q

Queenie (f.) This was given as a pet name to girls christened Regina, which is Latin for "queen." When Queen Victoria came to the throne, it was given as an independent name in her honor. Queen is the short form.

Quentin (m.) From the Latin, "fifth," it used to be given to the fifth-born child, if male, or fifth son. It is now given independently. It fell out of use after the Middle Ages but was reintroduced when Sir Walter Scott's novel *Quentin Durward* was published in 1823. It can also be spelled Quenton or Quinton.

Quincy (m.) Transferred use of a last name, from a French place name.

R

Rabbie (m.) Scottish pet form of Robert, usually associated with the poet Robert Burns (1759-96). The short form is Rab.

Rachel (f.) From the Hebrew, "ewe," an animal associated with gentleness and innocence. Rachel was the wife of Jacob, who labored for seven years to win her. This was a very popular name with the Puritans in the 17th century and also with the Victorians. It can be spelled Rachael, and the short forms are Rae, Ray, Rach and Rachie. Raquel is the Spanish form, made famous by the film star Raquel Welch.

Raisa (f.) Russian, from the Greek, "adaptable." Made famous by the wife of the Soviet leader, Mikhail Gorbachev.

Ralph (m.) From the Old English, "wolf counsel." Rafe

was the common 17th-century form of the name, and this pronunciation of Ralph is still occasionally heard in Britain, where the name was popular earlier this century. The spelling Rafe is now unusual.

Ramsay (m.) Transferred use of the Scottish last name, originally an English place name.

Randal (m.) From the Old English, "shield" and "wolf," it is a medieval version of Randolph, and many last names derive from it. Randy is the American short form, used as a name in its own right.

Randolph (m.) This is an 18th-century coinage from the same source as Randal. It can also be spelled Randolf.

Raoul (m.) The French equivalent of Ralph ("wolf-counsel"), it came to Britain with the Norman Conquest, but fell out of use there until it was revived in the 20th century.

Raquel *see* Rachel

Rastus (m.) Biblical: a convert of St. Paul's. The name comes from the Greek, "to love." This century it has been adopted by African-Americans.

Raymond (m.) From two Old German words, "counsel" and "protection," this name went to Britain with the Norman Conquest, but fell out of favor until the early years of this century. The short form is Ray, and this is occasionally given as an independent name. It can also be spelled Rae.

Rebecca (f.) Biblical: Rebecca married Isaac and bore Esau and Jacob. The name is of uncertain derivation, but could come from the Hebrew, meaning "knotted cord" or "noose." The quality of holding fast signified a faithful wife. It has always been well loved and was given a particular boost this century by Daphne du Maurier's 1938 novel of that name. The short form is Becky.

Reg, Reggie *see* Reginald

Regina (f.) From the Latin, "queen". A pet name is Queenie, and it can also be shortened to Gina and Rena.

Reginald (m.) From the same source as Reynold ("power" and "force"), this name fell out of use after the 15th century until it was revived in the 19th. The short forms are Reg, Reggie and Rex.

Renée (f.) French, meaning "reborn"; it was occasionally used by the Puritans in the 17th century and enjoyed a modest revival in the early years of the 20th. Renata and Renate are alternative forms, and René is the masculine. Sometimes the name is spelled Rennie or Renny.

Reuben (m.) Biblical: one of the twelve sons of Jacob, and thus a founder of one of the twelve tribes of Israel. It comes from the Hebrew, meaning "behold, a son." Perennially popular with Jewish families.

Rex (m.) From the Latin, "king," and also a pet form of Reginald. A 19th-century name.

Reynold (m.) From the Old English, "power" and "force," it was in frequent use up until the 15th century, when Reginald took over from it.

Rhett (m.) A name coined by Margaret Mitchell for her novel *Gone With The Wind* (1936).

Rhiannon (f.) A 20th-century Welsh name, a Celtic goddess from medieval literature.

Rhoda (f.) From the Greek, "rose," this name is found in the New Testament and has been in use in Britain since the 17th century.

Rhodri (m.) Welsh, "wheel ruler." It was the name of a 9th-century Welsh king.

Rodney

Rhonda (f.) From the Welsh place name, Rhondda, a 20th-century name used in Britain and America.

Rhys (m.) From the Welsh, "rash." This is a popular name in Wales and has an anglicized form, Rees.

Richard (m.) From the Old German, "stern ruler," introduced to Britain by the French at the time of the Norman Conquest. The name was given enormous appeal by Richard the Lionheart, leader of the Third Crusade. It has been shortened to Dick since the 13th century, and other short forms are Rich, Richie, Dickie, Rick, Ricky, Rikki, Ritchie and Dickon.

Rick *see* Richard

Rita (f.) A short form of Margarita, this became a name in its own right in the 20th century, and was given glamor by the film star Rita Hayworth (1918-87).

Robert (m.) From the Old German, "fame" and "bright." Robert is the French form, which supplanted the original Old English version after the Norman Conquest. The name has been a great favorite ever since. The short forms are Rob, Robbie, Rab and Rabbie (in Scotland), Bob and Bobby. A variant is Robin.

Roberta (f.) This is the feminine form of Robert, much used in Scotland. Robina, Robin, Robyn and Bobbie are also used for girls.

Rocky (m.) American, "tough guy." Rocky Marciano (1923-69), the champion boxer, made the name popular, as did the films of that name, which told the story of a prize fighter.

Roderick (m.) From the Old German, "fame" and "power." It is popular in Scotland, where it is used in place of an Old Gaelic name meaning "red," and in Wales, where it is used as an anglicized version of Rhodri. The short forms are Rod and Roddy.

Rodney (m.) From the last name, meaning "reed island," this became a first name in honor of Admiral Lord Rodney, who defeated the French in 1760. Now fairly common, it has the short forms Rod and Roddy.

Roger (m.) From the Old English, "fame" and "spear," the present form was introduced with the Norman Conquest and has been a favorite ever since. Rodge is the pet form.

Roland (m.) From the Old German, "fame" and "land," the present form was introduced to Britain by the Normans. It was the name of a colleague of Charlemagne, who is the subject of the *Chanson de Roland*. Rowland is an alternative spelling, and Rolando and Orlando are Italian forms sometimes used. Rolo and Roly are the short forms.

Rolf (m.) From the same source as Ralph ("wolf counsel"), this name came to Britain with the Norman Conquest, but soon lost popularity to Ralph. It was revived in the late 19th century. Rollo is the pet form.

Ronald (m.) Derives from the same source as Reginald ("power" and "force"). It was especially popular during Ronald Reagan's presidency. The short forms are Ron and Ronnie.

Ronan (m.) From the Gaelic, "seal" (the animal), it was borne by several early Celtic saints.

Rory (m.) From the Gaelic, meaning "red" or "ruddy," it was the name of a 12th-century king of Ireland, and is particularly popular today there and in Scotland. It can also be a short form of Roderick.

Rosalie (f.) From the Latin, referring to a festival called *rosalia*, at which garlands of roses were draped on tombs. Rosalia is the earlier version of the name, and Rosaleen is an Irish alternative.

Rosalind (f.) From the Old German, "horse serpent," though the Spanish language puts a different interpretation on it: "pretty rose." It was given by Shakespeare to his heroine in *As You Like It*. Rosaline, Roslyn and Rosalyn are alternative forms.

Rosamund (f.) Originally from the Old German, "horse protection," though in the Middle Ages it was associated with the Latin, "pure rose," or "rose of the world," both titles given to the Virgin Mary. Rosamond is an alternative spelling, and the short forms are Rose, Roz and Rozzie.

Rose (f.) Associated always with the flower, and therefore very popular, this name actually came from the Old German, meaning "horse." It went to England with the Norman Conquest, and has many variations, including Rosa, Rosabel, Rosabella, Rosanne, Rosanna, Rosina, Rosita and Rosetta. The pet forms, also used as independent names, are Rosebud, Rosie and Rosy.

Rosemary (f.) The name of the plant, or the combination of the two popular names Rose and Mary, this has the Latin meaning "dew of the sea." Its popularity has increased over the last two centuries. It can also be spelled Rosemarie, and the short forms are Rose, Rosie and Romy.

Ross (m.) From the Gaelic, "peninsula," this has been transferred from a last name to a first name and is particularly popular in Scotland.

Rowan (m. and f.) This comes from the Irish, meaning "little red-haired one," and also from the tree of that name, which is thought to have the power to drive away the devil. It is given to both girls and boys.

Rowena (f.) Coming from the Welsh, "slender blade," this name gained popularity when it was used by Sir Walter Scott in his novel *Ivanhoe* (1819). A short form is Rona, though this is the name of two Scottish islands and used also in its own right.

Rowland *see* Roland

Roxanne (f.) The name of the wife of Alexander the Great, this comes from the Persian meaning "dawn." Roxanne was the beloved of *Cyrano de Bergerac*, and Daniel Defoe wrote a novel of this name (1724) in which Roxanne was a beautiful courtesan who enjoyed a brilliant career but ended her days penniless in jail. It can also be spelled Roxane and Roxana.

Roy (m.) From the Gaelic, "red," but sometimes taken to be from the French, meaning "king." Rob Roy, the famous 18th century Scottish leader, was so known because of his red hair, and the name was given a further boost by Sir Walter Scott's novel about him (1817). It is particularly popular in Scotland.

Royston (m.) Transferred use of the last name, from an English place name.

Roz *see* Rosamund

Ruby (f.) One of a group of jewel names introduced in the late 19th century, it is now out of fashion.

Rudolf (m.) From the Old German, "fame" and "wolf," the name was given currency in the late 19th century by Anthony Hope's books *The Prisoner of Zenda* and *Rupert of Hentzau*, in which Rudolph Rassendyll is the main character. It was given a further boost by the film star Rudolf Valentino (1895-1926), a famous screen lover. It is now out of fashion. The short form is Rudy, and the name can also be spelled Rudolph.

Rufus (m.) From the Latin, "red-haired," famous as the nickname of William the Conqueror's son, William Rufus, who became William II. Now used often in America.

Rupert (m.) From the same source as Robert, this name means "bright fame." Prince Rupert of the Rhine (1618-92) came to England to support his uncle, Charles I, and the Royalist cause and was much admired for his courage and daring. It was fashionable to name boys in his honor. The British poet Rupert Brooke, who died in World War I, was another Rupert to catch parents' imagination.

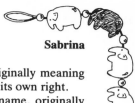

Sabrina

Russ (m.) Short form of Russell, and originally meaning "red," this has now become a name in its own right.

Russell (m.) Transferred use of the last name, originally meaning "little red one," it came into use in the 19th century and may have been bestowed recently in honor of the philosopher Bertrand Russell (1872-1970), champion of pacifism and nuclear disarmament. The short forms are Rusty and Russ.

Ruth (f.) Possibly from the Hebrew, "compassion," Ruth gave her name to a book in the Bible in which she is portrayed as being faithful and devoted. Ruthie is the pet form. It is one of the biblical names that were adopted by the Puritans in the 17th century, and it has never gone out of fashion.

Ryan (m.) A transferred use of the Irish last name, this is of obscure meaning. It has been adopted enthusiastically by parents in Britain, America and Australia. Ryan O'Neal (b.1941), the film actor, is a famous bearer of the name.

S

Sabina (f.) From the Latin, meaning "Sabine woman." The Sabine women were famous for having made peace with the Romans after the Romans abducted them, and their own men came to take revenge. The masculine form is Sabin, which has not survived, but the French feminine form, Sabine, is sometimes used.

Sabrina (f.) The Latin name of the river Severn, which was called after a legendary Celtic heroine, the illegitimate daughter of a Welsh king, who was drowned in the river on the orders of the queen. Popular in the U.S., it is shortened to Brina or Brie.

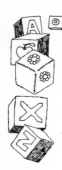

Sacha

Sacha (m. and f.) This is one of the Russian names that were introduced into the U.S. by Diaghilev's Ballet Russe in the early years of this century. It is the short form of the Russian for Alexander ("defender of men"), and used in the English-speaking world for both boys and girls. It can also be spelled Sasha.

Sadie (f.) Originally a pet form of Sarah, this is now a name in its own right.

Saffron (f.) A crocus with valuable golden stamens used as a cooking spice and a fabric dye; this became a fashionable name in the 20th century.

Sally (f.) Originally a pet name for Sarah, this has been used independently for about 200 years, and has its own short form, Sal. It can also be spelled Sallie. It is sometimes used in compound names such as Sally Ann.

Sam *see* Samantha, Samuel

Samantha (f.) Of unknown origins, it seems to have been coined in the 18th century in America. The 20th century has seen it rise to great popularity all over the English-speaking world. Its short forms are Sam and Sammy.

Samuel (m.) Biblical: Samuel was a Hebrew judge who anointed King Saul and King David after him. It was popular among the Puritans of the 17th century, and has always been a favorite Jewish name. It is currently enjoying a popularity, especially in its short form Sam. Another pet form is Sammy. The original Hebrew meaning of the name was "God has heard."

Sandra (f.) The short form of the Italian name Alessandra, this became popular after the publication of George Meredith's novel *Sandra Belloni* (1886). An alternative spelling is Zandra, and the pet forms are Sandy and Sandie.

Sandy *see* Alexander, Sandra

Sarah (f.) From the Hebrew, "princess," Sarah was the wife of Abraham in the Old Testament. It has been very popular since the 17th century and is still well liked today. It has been shortened to Sairey and Sarey and can be spelled Sara. Zara is an alternative form, and Sally the pet name.

Sasha *see* Sacha

Saskia (f.) This is a Dutch name of obscure origin and was borne by the wife of Rembrandt, who painted her often.

Saul (m.) This is a biblical name: Saul of Tarsus was converted on the road to Damascus and became St. Paul. It comes from the Hebrew, meaning "asked for." It was in use in Britain in the 17th century, but is now usually found only in Jewish families.

Scarlett (f.) Scarlett O'Hara is the heroine of Margaret Mitchell's novel *Gone with the Wind* (1936); this is one of a group of names invented by that author which took hold in the real world.

Scott (m.) Transferred use of the last name, meaning "a Scot." It was famously borne by the American writer F. Scott Fitzgerald (1896-1940).

Seamus *see* James

Sean (m.) The Irish form of John ("God is gracious"), it can also be spelled Shaun or Shawn. Its popularity has spread beyond Ireland and it is now commonly used throughout the English-speaking world. An American variant is Shane, which was made popular by the movie Western of that name.

Sebastian (m.) Latin, "man of Sebastia," a town in Asia Minor which derives its name from the Greek, "venerable," or "majestic." St. Sebastian was a Roman soldier

who was murdered by the arrows of his fellow officers, and this scene has been the subject of many paintings. The short form Bastian became a regional British name, but it is only in this century that Sebastian has caught on significantly. Seb (as in the athlete Seb Coe) and Sebby are the common short forms.

Selina (f.) Of uncertain origin, though it may come from the name of a Greek moon goddess, Selene, or from the medieval name Celina, which was derived from the Latin, "heaven." It is a name that has become popular in the 1980s.

Selma (f.) Of disputed origin, this may come from the Arabic, "peace." It was the name of Ossian's castle in the 18th-century poems of James Macpherson. A variant is Selima.

Selwyn (m.) Transferred use of the last name, it could come from the Old English, "prosperous friend." It was taken up as a first name by the Welsh in the 19th century.

Serena (f.) The feminine form of the Latin, "calm," "serene," this was the name of an early Christian saint.

Seth (m.) The third son of Adam, born after Cain murdered Abel. It was popular in the 17th century, particularly with parents who had previously lost a child, but then fell out of favor. It is recently enjoying a comeback.

Shamus *see* James

Shane *see* Sean

Shannon (f.) The name of the Irish river, this is used not in Ireland, but in America, where it has become very popular of late.

Sharon (f.) In the Bible this is the name of a fertile plain of great natural beauty. It has become very popular as a first name this century, and variants are Sharron, Sharona and Sharonda.

Shaun *see* Sean

Shawn *see* Sean

Sheila (f.) This is the English pronunciation of the Gaelic name Sile, which comes from Celia ("heavenly"). In

Ireland it is often spelled Shelagh. In Australia it has been the slang term for a woman since the 19th century.

Shelley (f.) A transferred use of the last name, which means "clearing on a slope," it became popular for boys in honor of the poet Percy Bysshe Shelley (1792-1822). As a pet form of Michelle, Rachel and Shirley, it is also given to girls. From the 1940s it has been exclusively a girl's name. Shell is the short form.

Sheree (f.) From the French, *chérie*, "darling," this is particularly popular in America, spelled Sherry, but can also be spelled Cherie, Sheri and Sherri. Sherena is a variant and the name can also form compounds, such as Sheri Ann.

Sheridan (m.) Transferred use of the last name most famously borne by the Irish playwright Richard Brinsley Sheridan (1751-1816). It is also occasionally used as a girl's name.

Sherman (m.) Transferred use of the last name from the Old English for "shears man," someone who trimmed cloth after it had been woven. Popular in America.

Shifra (f.) From the Hebrew, "beauty," "grace." It was traditionally the name of a midwife who disobeyed King Herod's orders to kill all baby boys.

Shirley (f.) Originally a last name, from a place name meaning "shire meadow," it was taken by Charlotte Bronte to be a girl's name for her novel *Shirley* (1849). It became widely popular with the fame of the child movie star Shirley Temple (b.1928). Short forms are Shirl, Shell and Shelley.

Sian (f.) A Welsh form of Jane ("God is gracious"), made well known by the actress Sian Phillips.

Sibyl (f.) This was the Greek word for a prophetess and went to Britain with the Normans. The spelling has always been problematical, even in classical times, and the alternative Sybil is as often used. Sybille, Sibyll, Sybilla and Sibylla are also found.

Sidney (m. and f.) Transferred use of the last name, from the French place name St. Denis, or from the Old English, "wide meadow." In Ireland and America it is used primarily as a feminine name, as it was in 18th-century England. It can also be spelled Sydney, and the short form is Sid.

Sidony (f.) From Sidonia, "woman of Sidon," this has the French form Sidonie. Sidney used as a girl's name is sometimes taken to be a contraction of Sidony.

Siegfried (m.) From the Old German, "victory" and "peace." It was popular during the Middle Ages and enjoyed a revival in the 19th century because of Wagner's music. Siegfried Sassoon (1886-1967), the poet, was a famous bearer of the name. The pet form is Sigi.

Sigmund (m.) From the Old German, "victory protector"; a famous modern bearer of this name has been the father of psychoanalysis, Sigmund Freud.

Sigrid (f.) A Scandinavian name, "fair victory," this has recently been adopted by English-speaking parents.

Silas (m.) Biblical, a companion of St. Paul; the name is short for Silvanus, and comes from the Greek, "wood." Silvana is the feminine form.

Silvester (m.) From the Latin, "of the woods"; the name

was borne by several early saints and three popes. It has been used from the Middle Ages right up to the present day, though it is by no means common. It can also be spelled Sylvester.

Simeon (m.) Biblical, with the Hebrew meaning "listening," it has the same origins as Simon. Simeon was the old man who blessed the baby Jesus in the Temple. It was used in Britain in the Middle Ages, but is rare today.

Simon (m.) The popular form of the name Simeon, it was much used in the Middle Ages when Simon Peter (St. Peter) had a great following, but fell out of favor during the Reformation because of its association with Roman Catholicism. It is quite frequently used again today.

Simone (f.) The French feminine form of Simon, this is gaining currency with American and British parents.

Sinclair (m.) Transferred use of the Scottish last name, from the French place name St. Clair, this was first used as a given name this century.

Sindy *see* Cindy

Sinead (f.) Irish Gaelic form of Janet, from Jane ("God is gracious").

Siobhan (f.) The popular Irish form of Joan ("God is gracious"). Anglicized spellings are Shevaun, Shavon, Shevon and Chevonne, which reflect the pronunciation.

Solomon (m.) From the Hebrew, "little man of peace." King Solomon was the son of King David, famed for his wisdom and his Song of Songs. The name was used in the Middle Ages and revived by the Puritans, but is not particularly popular today outside Jewish families. Solly is the short form.

Sonia (f.) Russian pet form of Sophia. It became popular in the English-speaking world this century, and can be spelled Sonya and Sonja.

Sophie (f.) A pet form of Sophia. It was popular in the 18th century and has found great favor with parents recently. It comes from the Greek, meaning "wisdom." It can also be spelled Sophy.

Spencer

Spencer (m.) Transferred use of the last name, which originally came from the office of "dispenser" of supplies in a great household. It was Sir Winston Churchill's second name and made famous also by the film star Spencer Tracy (1900-67).

Stacy (f. and m.) Originally the short form of either Anastasia ("insurrection") or Eustacia, this has become a name in its own right and is particularly popular in North America. Stacie and Stacey are the other forms.

Stanley (m.) Transferred use of the last name, from the Old English place name, "stony field," it was first adopted as a given name in the 19th century. It became particularly popular after Dr. Livingstone's meeting with the explorer H.M.Stanley. After flourishing in the early years of this century it has fallen into decline. The short form is Stan.

Stefan (m.) The form of Stephen found in Germany, Scandinavia, Russia and Poland, and occasionally used by English-speaking parents.

Stella (f.) Latin, "star." It was first used in Britain in the 16th century by the poet Sir Philip Sidney in *Astrophel and Stella*. Alternative forms are Estelle, Estrella and Estella.

Stephanie (f.) The feminine form of Stephen, it appeared this century and has been very popular. Princess Stephanie of Monaco keeps the name in the public eye. Short forms are Steph, Stephie, Steffi and Steff.

Stephen (m.) From the Greek, "crown" or "wreath." The name of several saints, it was borne by the first Christian martyr, who is celebrated on 26 December. It was common in Britain before the Norman Conquest and has remained popular. Steven is the alternative spelling, though Stefan is also coming into use. Steve and Stevie are the short forms.

Stewart *see* Stuart

St. John (m.) The name of the saint, and favored by Roman Catholic families, this is pronounced "Sinjun," and has been in use particularly in Britain, for the past 200 years.

84

Tallulah

Stuart (m.) Transferred use of the Scottish last name, it originally denoted the office of a person who looked after animals bred for the table. It was the name of the royal house of Scotland, and is now popular throughout the English-speaking world. A variant spelling is Stewart and the short forms are Stu, Stew and Stewie.

Susan, Susanna (f.) From the Hebrew for "lily," Susanna was the first form of this name to be used in the English-speaking world, where it was introduced during the Middle Ages. Susan came into use in the 18th century and by the 19th had ousted the earlier form almost completely. Variants are Suzan, Suzannah, Suzanne and Suzette. The short forms are Sue, Susie and Suzy.

Sybil *see* Sibyl

Sydney *see* Sidney

Sylvester *see* Silvester

Sylvia (f.) From the Latin, "wood." It was mainly used by poets until it caught the imagination of parents earlier this century. It can also be spelled Silvia, and the pet French form, Sylvie, has recently been adopted as a name in its own right.

T

Tabitha (f.) From the Aramaic, "gazelle"; Tabitha (called Dorcas in Greek) was a woman whom St. Peter restored to life. The name was very popular with the Puritans of the 17th century, and can also be spelled Tabatha.

Taffy *see* David

Tallulah (f.) From the Gaelic, "princess," this is also the Native American name of the Tallulah Falls in Georgia. It was famously borne by the actress Tallulah Bankhead (1903-68).

Tamara

Tamara (f.) A Russian name, this comes from the Hebrew, "date palm." The river Tamar, which runs between Devon and Cornwall, may also have helped its popularity in recent years.

Tammy (f.) This pet form of Thomasina, Tamara and Tamsin became a name in its own right, boosted by a film and a song of the same name in the 1950s. Popular in America.

Tamsin (f.) This was originally a pet form of Thomasina ("twin"), but when that fell out of favor, Tamsin was used as an independent name in Cornwall. It came back into fashion this century.

Tansy (f.) From the Greek, "immortal," and also from the flower of that name. It is gaining popularity, though still unusual.

Tanya (f.) The short form of the Russian name Tatiana, which is the name of various early saints, and comes from a Roman family name. Tanya can also be spelled Tania.

Tara (f.) This comes from the Irish, "crag," and was first used as a given name this century in the U.S. It soon became popular in Britain, too.

Tarquin (m.) Probably from an Etruscan family name, this was borne by two early Roman kings.

Tawny (f.) Like Ginger and Sandy, this name may be used to denote coloring or warmth of character.

Ted, Teddy *see* Edward, Edmund, Theodore

Terence (m.) Of unknown meaning, this was a Roman family name. It came to Britain from Ireland, where it is very popular, also in its short form, Terry. Tel is another nickname.

Teresa (f.) The origins of this name have been lost, though it first became widely used in Spain, where it was well known from St. Teresa of Avila in the 16th century. Theresa is the alternative spelling, and the French form, Thérèse, has also been adopted by English-speaking parents. Terry and Teri are the pet forms.

Tess, Tessa (f.) These began as short forms of Teresa, but are now more often used in their own right. Tess was given a great boost by Thomas Hardy's novel, *Tess of the d'Urburvilles*. Tessie is a pet form.

Thaddeus (m.) This is possibly from the Greek, "gift of God," and is generally a choice of Irish parents.

Thea (f.) The short form of Dorothea and of Theodora, this is also used as an independent name.

Thelma (f.) This name was first coined by Marie Corelli for her novel *Thelma* (1887), after which it caught on rapidly throughout the English-speaking world.

Theodore (m.) From the Greek, "gift of God," it was borne by several early saints and has the feminine form Theodora. The short forms are Teddy in America and Theo in Britain. The Welsh version is Tudor. Its popularity in the United States was helped by President Theodore Roosevelt, and the teddy bear was named after him because he was a keen hunter.

Thomas (m.) From the Aramaic, "twin." The 12th-century St. Thomas à Becket made the name widespread in Britain, and it has always remained very popular, enjoying a particular upsurge today. The short forms are Tom (often used independently) and Tommy. Thomasina is the feminine form, which has practically disappeared from use. The nickname for a British soldier is Tommy because in the 19th century the enlistment forms featured the specimen signature of Private Tommy Atkins.

Thora (f.) From the Norse for "dedicated to Thor," the god of thunder.

Tiffany (f.) This comes from the Greek, "epiphany," which

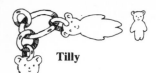

Tilly

means "appearance of God." It used to be given to girls born on the Feast of Epiphany (6 January), but is now used independently, and is enjoying popularity at present.

Tilly *see* Matilda

Timothy (m.) From the Greek, "honor God." The name of a companion of St. Paul, it was not used in Europe until the 16th century, but is quite a favorite in Britain and Ireland today.

Tina (f.) This was originally a short form of names such as Christina, but is now used independently.

Toby (m.) Short form of Tobias, from the Hebrew, "God is good."

Todd (m.) Transferred use of the last name, originally a dialect word for "fox," which is popular in the U.S. and Australia. It can also be spelled Tod.

Tom *see* Thomas

Toni, Tony *see* Anthony

Topaz (f.) A modern gemstone name.

Tracy (f.) This was formerly a masculine name, transferred from the last name, originally a French place name. Sometimes it is taken to be a short form of Teresa. It has been extremely popular over the past couple of decades, but is now falling out of fashion.

Travis (m.) Transferred use of the last name, originally a French name, from the verb meaning "to cross," and thus "crossroads." It was probably given to toll collectors. It is particularly popular as a first name in North America and Australia.

Trevor (m.) Transferred use of the Welsh last name, from the Welsh place name, meaning "large settlement." The Welsh form is Trefor. It has been very popular in recent years and has the short form Trev.

Tricia *see* Patricia

Tristram (m.) The tragic hero of the medieval love story of Tristram and Isolde, the name could come from the Celtic, "tumult," or the French, "sad." Tristan is a variant, as is Tristran.

Trixie *see* Beatrice

Troy (m.) The name of the ancient city in Asia Minor which the Greeks besieged for 10 years to win back the beautiful Helen for her husband. It has been used by parents over the past couple of decades.

Trudy *see* Gertrude

Tyrone (m.) The name of the Irish county, which means "Owen's county." Tyrone Power and Tyrone Guthrie were two famous theatrical bearers of the name.

Una (f.) This is an Irish name of uncertain derivation, which can also be spelled Oonagh or Oona. The Latin meaning of the name is "one," and it may be taken by parents to be related to Unity. Una Stubbs, the actress, is a well known bearer of the name.

Ursula (f.) From the Latin, "little bear," it was the name of a 5th-century Cornish saint who was murdered along with her companions after a shipwreck. This century the film star Ursula Andress has kept the name in the public eye, though it remains an unusual choice.

V

Valentine (f. and m.) From the Latin, "healthy," "strong."
St. Valentine was a Roman priest of the 3rd century who
was martyred on February 14, which is the eve of the
festivities of the goddess Juno, when lots were drawn to
choose lovers. The two celebrations became amalga-
mated and in the 19th century St. Valentine's Day began
to be commercially exploited by card manufacturers.
Val is the short form.

Valerie (f.) From the Roman clan name, which originally
meant "to be in good health." Valeria was the Victorian
form, until Valerie arrived from France and superseded
it. It was very popular in the first half of the 20th century.
The short form is Val.

Van (m.) From the Dutch, this means "from" or "of." It
used to be merely the prefix to a last name, but now it
is given in its own right.

Vanessa (f.) A name coined by Jonathan Swift for his friend
Esther Vanhomrigh. It was very popular around the
middle of this century and is still going strong. The pet
forms are Ness and Nessie.

Vaughan (m.) Transferred use of the Welsh last name, from
the Welsh word for "small." Originally bestowed as a
nickname.

Velma (f.) A modern American name of uncertain origin,
possibly invented by the novelist Raymond Chandler.

Venetia (f.) The Latin name for the city of Venice.

Vera (f.) This could come from the Russian for "faith" or
the Latin for "true." It was popular in the early years of
the 20th century.

Verity (f.) One of the abstract names popular with the
Puritans in the 17th century.

Vernon (m.) Transferred use of the Norman last name,
originally meaning "alder grove." It came into fashion
in the 19th century.

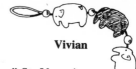

Vivian

Veronica (f.) From the Latin, "true image." St. Veronica was the name given to the woman who wiped Christ's face while he was on the road to Calvary and found his image printed on the cloth.

Victor (m.) From the Latin, "conqueror." The name of several early saints and a pope. It was not common in England until the reign of Queen Victoria, in whose honor it was often bestowed; since then its popularity has faded. The short forms are Vic and Vick.

Victoria (f.) From the Latin, "victory," this name was hardly used in Britain before Queen Victoria came to the throne in 1837, and after that it was normally given only as a second name. It became very popular this century. It is often met in its short form Vicky, which can also be spelled Vikki.

Vincent (m.) From the Latin, "conquering," it was borne by a 3rd-century saint. Though it was used in medieval England, it fell out of favor, only to be revived in the 19th century. The short form is Vince.

Viola, Violet (f.) Viola is Latin for "violet," the flower. Viola was used by Shakespeare in *Twelfth Night*, but never really caught on. Violet was enormously popular in the 19th century. Vi is the short form.

Virginia (f.) This comes from an ancient Roman clan name. It was bestowed by Sir Walter Raleigh on the colony he founded in America in honor of Queen Elizabeth I, the Virgin Queen, and it was given to the first American child of English parents to be born there. The short forms are Ginny and Gina.

Vita (f.) Sometimes used as a short form of Victoria (as for the English writer and gardener Vita Sackville-West, 1892-1962), this is also given as an independent name. It means "life" in Latin.

Vivian, Vivien (f. and m.) From the Latin, "alive." In Britain the first spelling is usually masculine, and the second feminine. Vivienne is an alternative feminine spelling. It was very popular in the 1950s, and the short form is Viv.

Wade (m.) From the Old English, "ford," this has been transferred from a last name to a first name in the U.S.

Wallace (m.) Transferred use of the Scottish last name, which was originally an Old French word, meaning "foreigner." It first became a given name in the 19th century. The alternative spelling, Wallis, is often used for girls in the U.S. and was the name of the late Duchess of Windsor.

Wally (m.) The short form of Walter or Wallace, this was also used in its own right until "wally" became slang in Britain for a stupid person.

Walter (m.) From the Old German, "rule" and "people," it became very popular after the Norman Conquest. Sir Walter Raleigh's son, who was named after him, was called Wat for short, and other short forms are Walt, Wal and Wally.

Wanda (f.) Of uncertain origin, it was popularized in 1883 by Ouida's novel of that name. Vanda is a variant.

Ward (m.) Transferred use of the last name, originally meaning "guard."

Warren (m.) From the Old German, "defender," or from the French place name, meaning "game park." It appeared mainly as a last name until the 19th century and has gained recent popularity because of the movie star Warren Beatty.

Warwick (m.) From the place name, which means "houses by the weir."

Wayne (m.) Transferred use of the last name, from the Old English denoting the occupation cartwright. Its recent popularity is probably due to the fame of movie star John Wayne (1907-79).

Wendy (f.) This name was coined by J.M. Barrie for *Peter Pan* in 1904. It came from a childish attempt to say "friend" – "fwendy." Its appeal to parents was immediate and it achieved great popularity in the first half of the century; it is now less common.

Wesley (m.) From the Old English, "west meadow." It was the last name of the founder of the Methodist Church, John Wesley (1703-91), and it became a first name in his honor. Wes is the short form.

Whitney (f. and m.) Transferred use of the last name, originally meaning "by the white island," this is popular in America, and pop singer Whitney Houston has made it widely known.

Wilbur (m.) From the Old German for "will" and "defense." Orville and Wilbur Wright were the pioneer aviators, making their first flight in 1903.

Wilfred (m.) From the Old German for "will" and "peace." In the 7th century St. Wilfrid (alternative spelling) made the name popular in the North of England, where he preached. It fell out of favor but was revived in the 19th century. The short form is Wilf.

William (m.) From the Old German for "resolution" and "helmet," it was brought to England by the Normans and was the most common of all masculine names until John superseded it in the 13th century. It continued to be widely used until recently. Just when it was falling out of favor, the present Prince and Princess of Wales gave it to their eldest son (b.1982), thus assuring its continued popularity. The short forms are Will, Bill and Billy, and Liam is an Irish version. Wilhelmina, Willa and Wilma are used for girls, with the short forms Minnie and Minna.

Winifred (f.) From the Welsh name, meaning "friend of

peace." There was a 7th-century saint of this name, but it did not become popular until the 16th century. Win, Wyn, Winnie and Freda are all short forms.

Winston (m.) Originally a place name, meaning "Wine's farm," it became a last name and was taken up as a first name in the Churchill family in the 17th century. In recent times it has been given in honor of Prime Minister Winston Spencer Churchill (1874-1965).

X

Xanthe (f.) From the Greek, "yellow." An unusual choice.

Xavier (m.) From the Arabic, "bright," it was made popular by the 16th-century Saint Francis Xavier. Xaviera is the feminine form.

Xenia (f.) From the Greek, "guest." It can also be spelled Zenia, as it is pronounced.

Y

Yasmin *see* Jasmine

Yehudi (m.) From the Hebrew, "praise," famous from the violinist Yehudi Menuhin.

Yolanda (f.) From the Greek, "violet flower." Iolanthe is an alternative form, and Yolande is the French.

Yvonne, Yvette (f.) From the same root as the French boy's name Yves, meaning "yew."